Woven Yarns

Vol.1

Woven by Nora Curran

Dedication

I dedicate these stories to the memory of my husband, John Davidson Curran.

Acknowledgments

These stories have been woven together with the help of my Creative Writers' group in La Mesa, California.

Special thanks to Lisa Climenson, and Susan Bodinet.

I also want to thank Susan Baris of Amazon Publishing Groups for her patience and care with edits and suggestions for improvements to both content and appearance.

About the Author

Nora Curran is a globetrotting storyteller born on the enchanting Mediterranean island of Cyprus. She was educated in England and worked for the BBC World Service for many years. She came to roost in the US via Beijing, London and eHarmony. Nora has woven the rich experiences garnered from her travels and adventures into the narrative fabric of her work. She is a linguist and wordsmith. She lived in Hong Kong during its colonial era and then returned to China in the 21st century to observe its changing landscape. These threads have profoundly influenced her perspective on culture and identity. She describes herself as a maverick and a nomad.

In her memoir, "Tapestry of a Life – An Odyssey Spanning Three Continents", Nora invited readers into her diverse journey, and now she returns with her thought-provoking new series, "Woven Yarns". This two-volume collection of stories intricately fuses social commentary with fictionalized realities, offering a unique lens on contemporary issues such as climate change, the complexities of cultural adaptation, the risks of internet dating, and the weight of caregiving, all while embracing the enchanting unpredictability of life.

When she's not capturing the essence of the human experience through her writing, Nora enjoys weaving, painting, and observing the fascinating tapestry of humanity. Now residing in the USA, she cherishes her time with friends and kindred spirits as she continues to travel the world in search of inspiration. She lives in San Diego which she calls home.

Table of Contents

Preface

Weaving, like pottery, is one of the most ancient of crafts. It's the interlacement of threads to create fabric. I was introduced to weaving by my husband, John, who was a master weaver. I watched mesmerized as he passed the shuttle from one end of the loom to the other as he created beautiful patterns.

In the intricate weaving of life, each thread tells a story, and each story contributes to the rich tapestry of our existence. "Woven Yarns" invites you to embark on a journey through the threads that have been woven on the loom of my life—interlaced with a lifetime of experiences, travels, memories, and imagination.

Born on the sun-kissed shores of Cyprus and educated in England, I have had the immense privilege of traveling across all continents and experiencing the vibrant rhythms of diverse cultures. From the bustling streets of Hong Kong during its colonial era to navigating the complexities of modern-day Beijing, my path has been colored by a multitude of encounters, each adding depth and texture to the fabric of who I am.

This collection of stories is a reflection of those lived experiences—a blend of social commentary, fictionalized truths, with a good sprinkling of humor. These yarns reveal the beauty and challenges of our shared human condition. The narratives within "Woven Yarns" are not merely recollections but rather threads that intertwine, capturing the essence of climate change, the perils of modern romance, and the profound responsibility of caring for our loved ones. Each story is woven to spark dialogue and inspire reflection in a world where connection is increasingly vital yet often elusive.

As a linguist and storyteller, I have sought to translate the complexities of life into narratives that resonate. Just as weaving requires patience and creativity, so does the art of storytelling. It is an exploration of how threads of joy, sorrow, hope, and resilience create a tapestry that reflects the diverse experiences of humanity.

I invite you to explore these "Woven Yarns," to unravel the stories that have shaped me and, perhaps, to find echoes of your own journey woven within the fabric. Let us celebrate the connections that unite us, the struggles that challenge us, and the beauty of life's unpredictable yet exquisite design.

Welcome to the adventure.

My Friend Gloria

An expectant hush fell over the courtroom as jurors returned to their seats. The criminal trial had lasted several weeks. The judge asked them if they had reached a unanimous decision. The foreperson said they had. A chill went down my spine.

I had sat in that courtroom for days, listening to prosecutors and defense lawyers examine and cross-examine witnesses. There was a strong chance that I, too, might be called to the witness box. The defense attorney asked me if I was willing to give evidence, and for some strange reason, I agreed and immediately regretted it. To my relief, my services were not needed. The local press took great interest in the case and covered it closely, keeping their readers up to date.

As I listened to the proceedings, my mind kept going back to the events that had led to this moment, searching for missed clues, trying to understand how I could have been so unaware or naive about human interactions. In my mind's eye, I was winding back the video to the time, seven years ago, when we came to live in this small town in California.

***

My husband Peter and I moved from Colorado to Southern California to be near our children and grandchildren. For years, our son and daughter had been asking us to relocate, but we were reluctant to make the move. The usual excuses prevailed: we had good jobs, wonderful friends and neighbors, a lively church, and the cost of living in Colorado was way below that of California. Of course, we missed the children and grandkids, but we were comfortably settled in our six-bedroom house in Aurora. During holidays, when the family got together, the kids usually came to us, since we had the most space. Peter never failed to tell them that we could never afford a six-bedroom house in San Diego.

"But, Dad, you won't need a six-bedroom house when you retire," they said.

"Your mom and I love to have lots of room. We can't be crammed in those tiny, boxy condos that pass for housing in your neck of the woods."

"This house is too big for you now. Why not downsize to something more manageable?" was their usual response.

We kept having this conversation every time we had a clan get-together.

For years, we kept telling ourselves that when we were done with our nine-to-five routines, we could travel and see the world. No more watching Rick Steves on TV enjoy the Greek Islands, visit castles in Europe, or describe the historic sights of Britain. We'd abandon those virtual tours with Rick Steves. Instead, with time on our hands, we could travel and see these places for ourselves—even venturing further afield and traveling to Bali, sailing down the Milford Sound in New Zealand, and walking on the Great Wall of China. There! Eat your heart out, Rick Steves!

By the time we eventually retired, Peter, a lifelong smoker, was diagnosed with stage three lung cancer. The doctor's diagnosis wiped out all those dreams. Any desire to see the pyramids in Egypt faded into insignificance. What we wanted and prayed for now was a miracle for Peter's health.

***

When we shared the news with our children, their pleas for us to move near them made sense. That's how we found ourselves living in a two-bedroom townhouse in San Diego County. Mercifully, Peter's cancer went into remission during the hectic and often traumatic move. He even started to plan activities and sightseeing trips.

Our new place consisted of three stories, and we shared walls on two sides with adjacent properties—all identical to ours. It was an age-restricted, active adult community of 20 houses. It was close to all amenities, especially the local hospital and doctors, which was handy for Peter's medical appointments.

Initial fears that we'd find it hard to adjust to our new surroundings were quickly dispelled by the warm reception we received from our neighbors, especially from the couple living next door, Ted and Gloria. They went out of their way to welcome us and make us feel at home. Not only did we share a wall, but also an interest in good food, music, art, and crafting.

Ted was originally from Chicago, the son of Italian immigrants who were in the restaurant business. He owned a gift shop offering a variety of items ranging from housewares and decorative objects, such as tea sets, kitchenware, and even some apparel. He named it "Pre-Owned New," with big bold lettering over the façade. He told us that we could have anything we needed from his shop at knockdown prices. Ted was in his mid-sixties and a trendy dresser. In the mornings, we'd see him leave for work looking dapper in a suit, tie, and highly polished shoes. He had jet-black hair—dyed, no doubt—and a gray mustache and beard. If you didn't know, you'd think he was a top executive going to a board meeting.

One day I asked him, "Where do you find such a great collection of new and nearly new items for your boutique?"

"Oh, I go up to LA twice a month, more often if there's a special on. I have some good contacts there."

"Well, I guess we're close enough to LA to make it worth your while. It's about a couple of hours 'drive from here, isn't it?"

"That's right if the traffic's light. LA is La-La Land," he said. "There are a lot of rich people around there who change and upgrade their homes and wardrobes as often as their underwear. You know, the Hollywood types. Film studios also get rid of unwanted stuff when they run out of storage space. I have a good nose for grabbing bargains," he said, tapping his nose and winking, obviously proud of his negotiating skills. It was true. Some of his stuff was brand new and high quality.

"I love those wooden figurines you have in your shop," I said.

"Oh really? I make them. That's my hobby, carving wood. When I'm not at the shop, I spend my time carving them at home. Gloria complains about the mess I make, but at the same time, she encourages me."

"What kind of wood do you use?"

"It's usually lime wood, also known as Basswood," and without any prompting from me, he launched into the intricacies of wood carving, the types of chisels, carving knives, and other tools he used. He said that Gloria always used birthdays and anniversaries as an excuse to buy him more wood and chisels. The following day, I found a small figurine I had previously admired on our doorstep. A gift from Ted.

Gloria, also in her mid-sixties, was petite and lithe. She had beautiful brown eyes, and I was sure that she was a regular gym visitor. She was the manager of the vitamin and health section in the local supermarket and extremely knowledgeable about natural remedies. Any time I was in the store, I noticed a long line of customers waiting to talk with her. I used to jokingly call her "Dr. Mercola." It wasn't long before I, too, started consulting her about minor ailments—headaches, aches, and pains—and she always came up with an appropriate homeopathic remedy.

"Here, take this for your pre-diabetic diagnosis," she said.

"What is it?"

"It's Cinnamomum cassia: cinnamon. Put two to three drops a day in a drink, but no more than three. Use the dropper."

I followed her advice, and my next blood test showed that my pre-diabetic condition had vanished.

For colds, she advised another herbal cure. "You have to hit it early. As soon as you feel a cold coming, take Origanum vulgare. It's a fancy name for oregano spirits." And it worked! It was like having a doctor living next door, always available with sound advice and no co-pay.

Peter and I agreed we were lucky to have such a nice, friendly couple next door. In some ways, I felt sad that they were not retired like us so that we could spend more time together.

It was selfish of me to think this way, but I always had at the back of my mind the fear that Peter's remission had an expiration date. How long would it last? Years? Weeks? For me, that was a constant. We also realized that our children were busy with their careers, children, and struggles. We didn't want to be a burden to them. It was important for us to make friends of our own, with whom we could share common interests and activities. Gloria and Peter fell in that category but were also busy with their respective jobs.

***

Meantime, we began exploring and familiarizing ourselves with San Diego. We went for drives into the hills, sat on the sand at Coronado Beach, and enjoyed drinks on the patio of Hotel Del. But somehow, I felt that these outings would be more enjoyable if shared with another couple.

I've always enjoyed cooking, but since Peter's illness, I was determined to cook good, nutritious meals using fresh ingredients. No more comfort foods or TV dinners. Gloria had great advice on various products, legumes, and the best way to prepare them. She told me to visit the local farmers 'market, where the produce is picked that very day. "You may have to pay a little bit more, but it's well worth it," she said.

As usual, she was right. On Fridays, I'd grab my big shopping bag, the one with wheels, and head for the farmers 'market, embarking on my culinary adventure. Our main street—closed to traffic that day—was filled with stalls selling not only produce but also freshly made pasta and cooked food. I soon got to know the vendors 'names and loved learning from them. As a city girl, I had never tasted heirloom tomatoes. Whenever I saw them in the store, I thought them ugly, but my new farmer friends urged me to taste them. I discovered there was quite a difference between a Roma and an heirloom tomato. The growers also shared the trials and tribulations of farming under capricious weather conditions, long droughts, fires, sudden floods, and hailstorms that could destroy an entire season's crop. We always ended up agreeing that it was all due to climate change.

***

Night Scene

During the warm, balmy California evenings, Peter and I often slept with our bedroom window open. One night, we were woken up by loud noises and police sirens. We both sat up in bed, wondering what had happened. We could hear voices and a lot of shouting but could not make out what was being said. I went to the window and peeped outside, willing the darkness to lift its veil.

"Stop trying to see through the blinds, Melissa. Get away from the window!" Peter warned. Although I usually went by Mel, when Peter was anxious or angry, he used my full name: Melissa.

"That's the last place to be if there's trouble."

He was right, of course, and before I went back to bed, I closed the window and locked it.

"I guess we'll find out what the fuss is about in the morning," I said, too tired to stay awake.

The following morning, we slept in and woke up tired. I put it down to the previous night's disturbance. As we sat on our front porch with our morning coffee, neighbor Jason came over from his place and said, "Did you hear the noise last night?"

"Yes, we did. Do you know what happened?"

"Oh, haven't you heard? The paramedics and police came. It was quite a ruckus."

"Was it the homeless guy again?" Peter asked.

"Hell no!" Jason said. "Ted beat Maisie's boyfriend to a pulp, and the police arrested him. The boyfriend's in the hospital."

Maisie and her boyfriend, Jon, lived in our community, a couple of condos to the left of us. They were both quiet, and we did not know them very well. They seemed to work long hours and were rarely home.

"What? You mean Ted, next door? Gloria's Ted?"

"Yep!" Jason nodded with a smug smile.

We were surprised—shocked. Jason had no idea who started the fight, but he was sure of the outcome: Ted was in jail, and Jon was in the hospital—Ted put him there.

I gulped down my coffee and headed to the store, hoping to talk to Gloria. I tried to catch her eye, but she was busy with customers and seemed distracted. This is not the appropriate time or place to ask about Ted. I'll catch up with her later. I left empty-handed and none the wiser. I was truly concerned for my friends. If Jason's story was true, it all seemed out of character. There had to be a good explanation.

The next couple of days passed without seeing Gloria or Ted, and we got busy with visitors from out of state. Our former Colorado neighbors and friends loved visiting and enjoying Coronado's sandy beaches. We were the excuse for their trips to the Golden State, and we also enjoyed catching up on news of our former neighborhood. The night "incident" slid into my memory's waiting room—the place where I put things for later.

***

Peter'S Cancer Returns

The day after our houseguests left, we got the devastating news that Peter's cancer had returned. I was heartbroken. The only consolation was that the kids were close by, but I knew that this was a battle Peter and I had to face together, and ultimately on my own.

I saw Gloria at the store that week, and she took one look and said, "Are you okay? What's wrong?"

Before I could stop myself, I burst into tears and shared the news with her.

She was genuinely upset too. "I'll come by after work," she said.

That evening, she visited with us. She tried to give us some hope: "You know, Peter can have more than one remission. I know people who have had several, and some can last a long time, even years. The main thing is to remain positive." She also suggested some supplements for him while undergoing chemotherapy but cautioned us to consult a doctor first.

Gloria was a tower of strength, and I got to know her better over the next few months. I learned that she and Ted had been high school sweethearts.

"I was divorced and had raised my son as a single mom. I don't know what made me do it, but I found him on Facebook as I searched for my high school friends. I found an old telephone number and tried it.

Imagine my surprise when he answered. We started talking, and finally, we got together. That was eight years ago."

"Wow! After how many years?" I said.

"It was twenty-five years later. By that time, we were both empty nesters. My son, Mike, had already bought his own house and had a great job, and Ted's children also were grown up and independent."

***

Christmas Scene

Christmas was approaching fast that year. Our children had booked a vacation in Honolulu and asked us to join them. We declined, preferring to stay home. We invited Gloria, Ted, and Jason with his wife, Myrtle, to join us for Christmas dinner.

Jason was chairman of our HOA board, and he always dealt promptly and efficiently with any issues that came up. His wife Myrtle was the kind of person you felt you could confide in, and that she'd sweep you up in her ample bosom and comfort you. She was a big woman with a gentle and kind face that inspired confidence—the motherly type. If you ever needed to find out what was going on in the neighborhood, she was the go-to person.

Since Ted was the only one who didn't drink alcohol, I stocked up on soft drinks as well. I was surprised, therefore, to see Gloria and Ted arrive with an open bottle of wine. "Here," Ted said, "let's start with this. It's a good red," and with that, he picked up a glass from the table and filled it. *He told me he never touches the stuff. Perhaps he's making an exception for Christmas.* He certainly was making up for lost time because he kept refilling his glass.

During the meal, I asked our guests if they could recall a Christmas or a holiday they had enjoyed in the past.

Ted was the first to respond. He started by saying, "Oh yes, I remember many holidays, but you have to be true to yourself. The most important thing is to be true to who you are. And to know who you are. That's important. You must fucking well have to know who you fucking are and what the fuck others want," and with that, he stood up and started to rant and rave, waving his glass of wine like a conductor's baton.

We all sat there stunned. Gloria tried to get him to sit down, but he simply ignored her—getting more and more agitated as his profanities grew stronger. His behavior became threatening, daring us to disagree or take him on. The room was blue with his vulgarity and swearing.

Eventually, Gloria managed to drag him away, and they left—Ted still mouthing threats and staggering as they went out the door.

"Well, that was a shock!" I said, trying to regain my composure. "I'm sorry about this. I can't understand what happened…"

I felt I had to apologize to Jason and Myrtle. Why, I didn't know. Perhaps for having invited Ted along with the others. "I don't know what to say."

"What brought this on?" Peter asked.

"Oh, I wouldn't feel bad about it," Jason said. "It's just Ted. That's his usual MO when he gets drunk."

"What do you mean, 'when he gets drunk?'" I said. "He told me he never touches the stuff."

Jason chuckled. "That's when he's on the wagon, which doesn't last long. He's more often in the weeds than on the wagon."

I had no idea. Peter and I had never seen him drunk or violent. I felt let down and disappointed.

"When he's sober, he's one of the nicest guys you can find. But when he drinks, he becomes violent. Don't you remember what he did to Maisie's boyfriend?"

That's when I recalled that night incident, a few months back, when we were awakened by shouting and police sirens. "What happened?" I asked. "We never found out what the fuss was about."

As HOA Board Chairman, Jason was bound to know what took place. He soon enlightened us. The police were called because two guys were fighting and causing a disturbance. It was a dark night, but the drunken brawl had woken several residents who called the police. The cops separated them. The two involved were Ted and Jon, Maisie's boyfriend, who also lived in our block. Jon was taken to the hospital as he was badly beaten up, and Ted to the police station. Gloria bailed Ted out the next day, and Jon took several weeks to recover from his injuries. Soon after that night, Maisie sold her condo, and both she and Jon moved away.

"I've had to warn Ted several times," Jason continued, "he's been rough and done some nasty things to people who cross him. The person who lived in your place before you had excrement plastered over her garage door."

"Our garage door?"

"Yes. The board had to get someone to power-wash it, and Ted was asked to pay. It was Gloria who paid because the bill went to her."

"You mean our current garage door?" I knew I was repeating myself, but I had to make sure.

"Yes. I've even told her that any more trouble from him, she'll be liable since the property is in her and her son's name."

I don't think I could ever again watch our garage door go up and down with the same nonchalance as before. I also started wondering about the thumps and noises we occasionally heard from Gloria's side of the wall.

"I'm worried for Gloria," Jason added, "living with a man who can turn violent and aggressive like that is not good. I've also seen her with the occasional black eye, and we wondered…"

"A few times I've seen her leave her house looking very upset," Myrtle chipped in. "I think she's having a hard time with him."

We were silent. This was a Dr. Jekyll and Mr. Hyde situation. How was it possible for one person to be both? Is that what they call split personality? No wonder it's called "demon drink."

"We all wish she'll have enough and get rid of him," Myrtle said.

"Men like that are not easy to kick out," I said, "she might be scared of what he might do. He won't leave voluntarily."

***

Peter Dies—I Move Away

That was our last Christmas together. Peter died peacefully at home the following March, and I moved to a one-story house down the street. The condo held too many sad memories, and my knees complained each time they met the stairs.

Not long after I settled into my new home, I got a call from Gloria. She had retired and asked if I was interested in being her walking buddy. She said she needed the exercise. "Strange you should call," I said, "I was just thinking the same thing. You must be a mind reader."

Gloria never tried to explain or apologize for the Christmas Day scene. After all, why should she? She wasn't the one who had exploded. Thankfully, I rarely saw Ted after that incident, and I was too busy and preoccupied caring for Peter during the last few months of his life.

I was pleased to hear from Gloria and rekindle our friendship. I realized that she was lonely and needed friends. Funny, I thought. I was the one needing friends when we first came here, but now, it's the other way around. I can never repay her for all her kindness and support she gave me in the past. I was also concerned for her, now that I knew how aggressive and foul-mouthed Ted could be.

Twice a week, we went for our early morning walks around town. She had lived in the area for many years as a single mother, raising her son Mike. She never mentioned his father, but I sensed that she was proud of the fact that she had raised a nice young man who was now an independent and successful businessman. At times, I wasn't sure whether she was proud of Mike for himself, or for the fact that she had raised him on her own and she deserved some credit for that. As I did not know the lad, I could not comment.

"You know, I've heard several stories of people who find former boyfriends or girlfriends via social media," I said to her during one of our walks. "I know of one other couple with a similar story. They knew each other in high school and then lost touch until thirty years later at a school reunion, by which time they were both widowed, with grown-up kids."

Gloria told me that she and Ted were high-school sweethearts and that their families expected them to marry after graduation. But for some reason, they went their separate ways, married other people, and raised families. Had it not been for that chance encounter on FB, they would never have gotten together. "Ted, coming back into my life, was like the completion of a circle. Something that started way back in high school is now coming round to full circle."

I didn't know how to respond to this.

"It was meant to be," she kept saying. "It was written in the stars."

Much as I enjoyed our walks together, this kind of talk made me feel uneasy. She was infatuated with him. Whenever I tried to suggest a new hobby or activity for her, the usual response was: "I think Ted would like that," or "I think Ted would be good at that. He's very artistic, and he'd enjoy that."

In the end, I gave up trying to coax her out of retirement. I didn't want to hear constantly about Ted and how wonderful or artistic he was. I never wanted to hear about Ted ever again.

Ted Makes Headlines Again

One Thursday morning, as I was getting ready to leave for our walk, Gloria called. "Can't walk today, I've got to go downtown!" With that, she abruptly hung up.

As I stood there trying to decide whether to walk solo or catch up on some other chores, my phone rang again. It was Myrtle. Agog with excitement, she screamed at eardrum-piercing volume: "Turn on the TV, channel five. Ted's made headlines again!" She too hung up.

I turned on the TV. There was Ted, in a rage, attacking people on the sidewalk. A small crowd surrounded him, and he kept lunging at them, shouting and daring them to take him on. A hapless youth stood to one side, leaning against the wall, filming it all on his cellphone. Ted went up to him, knocked the phone out of his hand, and punched him in the stomach. As the youth folded in two, Ted pushed him, and he fell to the ground. Ted stamped hard on the lad's phone, shouting threats and obscenities. My former neighbor was clearly drunk and behaving true to form.

I turned off the television. I had my own experience of Ted's drunken, violent behavior, and didn't need to see any more. Easier said than done. In a small town, an incident like this is a big story unless there's something more momentous taking place. For the next 24 hours, all the local radio stations, TV, newspapers, and social media kept replaying the scene, accompanied by various reports and speculation.

21

Later that evening, Myrtle called again to give me the skinny. A teen captured the whole episode on her cellphone.

"This young girl and her boyfriend were sitting in her car outside Ted's shop. Both were on the phone when suddenly they saw an attractive young woman run out of the shop followed by Ted."

I could hear the excitement in Myrtle's voice. She was gushing to tell me all the details, and there was no stopping her. "The woman went into Ted's shop and he started to pat her fanny. She asked him to stop, but he came onto her even stronger. She tried to leave, but he stood in the doorway blocking her exit."

As Myrtle was talking, I wondered about the young man who was knocked down and had his cellphone smashed.

"Somehow, the woman managed to escape and rushed out with Ted in hot pursuit. Feeling more confident out in the street, she turned around to confront him. It was quite a scene!"

"I guess that's when the two people in the car turned their phones around and took pictures of what was taking place," I said.

"Yes, but the boyfriend thought he'd get a better shot if he got out of the car. You saw what happened!"

"We both know how vicious Ted can be when he's drunk. Poor lad. Was he badly hurt?"

"I don't think so. I think his pride was hurt more than anything else. He was caught by surprise. The fact that an older man like Ted knocked him down in front of a crowd of people was humiliating for him."

"At least, the girlfriend had the sense to stay in the car, or else she too could have been hurt."

"Yes, but she kept filming, capturing the entire episode on her cellphone. Then posted it on social media. It went viral almost immediately."

"What happened to the woman who ran out of Ted's shop?" I asked.

"I don't know. I think she fled once Ted turned his attention elsewhere. She was wise not to hang around."

"I wonder how Gloria is coping with all this? The publicity must make her want to crawl into her shell and never come out," I said.

Myrtle chuckled. "Oh, she's got a hard shell, all right. She's put it all around her to ward off and immune herself from Ted's shameful behavior. You think she doesn't know?"

I wasn't so sure. Gloria must have been embarrassed by Ted's behavior.

"I know she's your friend," Myrtle continued, "but she could do a lot better than hitch her wagon to that loser. I think he's been fooling around with other women too. I saw them coming and going while Gloria was at work."

Inwardly, I agreed with Myrtle, but I felt some loyalty toward Gloria. I was aware of how unpopular and unwelcome Ted was in the community. I knew that his outbursts had alienated Gloria from her neighbors and friends. She had no social life at all, or any friends that I knew of. Her entire world revolved around Ted, his diet, his needs, and his moods. That was her life. I also sensed that Ted had alienated her son as well because I never saw him visit while we lived next door.

***

After her boyfriend hit the headlines, I did not know how to approach Gloria. I waited for her to call me, but the weeks went by, and there was no word from her. It would have been easy for me to give up on her, but I felt that her silence spoke of a rather sad, lonely woman who did not know how to reach out in her hour of need. I also missed those early morning walks and her company.

I let several weeks go by, and then I called her. Avoiding all mention of Ted's shenanigans, I asked if she'd be interested in resuming our walks.

She sounded pleased to hear from me and said she looked forward to starting our walks again. I was even more surprised when she did not shy away from mentioning the fact that Ted was on parole, waiting for his trial. "If he goes to jail, he goes to jail," she said and kept repeating it. She was matter-of-fact about it.

"When's the trial?" I asked.

"They haven't given him a date yet. The system's backed up. They have more serious cases to deal with first. This is small fry for them."

Not to the man who was attacked and had his cellphone smashed. I knew better than to ask who had put up the bail money.

"We were planning to go to Italy and visit the village where his family came from. A good thing we didn't commit and buy our tickets."

"I remember you telling me that money was tight. How come you're planning a trip to Italy?"

Gloria broke into my thoughts: "You know, we were going to get married after high school."

"Yes, you said. What happened?"

"My parents, my father mostly, put his foot down and said if I married him, he'd disinherit me and I would never see him again."

I wasn't surprised. I wouldn't want my daughter marrying someone like him.

***

We continued to meet at the end of my street for our morning walks. She moved with ease and confidence, and I suspected that at times she slowed down to give me time to catch my breath. She was more fit than I was. I resigned myself to the fact that part of the price I had to pay for her company was to listen to her talk incessantly about Ted and their history—past and present. It came out in small installments.

She told me that Ted's mother was an alcoholic and his father a jailbird. He was raised by an older sister and an uncle, who let Ted work and sleep in his Italian deli. He grew up in the Hull House neighborhood in Chicago's near West Side. That was in the fifties, before gentrification. He learned to take care of himself from a young age. Gloria told me that Ted's sister once said to her, "Try and keep him out of jail."

"Wow! That was prescient of her! Why did she say that?"

"They thought I was good for him and that I'd keep him on the straight and narrow. They welcomed me into their family and encouraged our relationship."

"Don't you think that was an unfair burden they put on you? Expecting you to take care of him and protect him from himself?"

"I don't know. They liked me, and I never thought of it like that. But now... now it looks as if he will go to jail," Gloria said.

"You can't blame yourself or feel guilty. He's only got himself to blame. He's lucky to have you in his life."

"And I'm lucky to have him in mine," she responded, which annoyed me intensely.

Can't she see what a dope he is and that he's using her? She interrupted my thoughts by saying, "It's the drink, you know. He's really kind and generous when he's not drinking. He's a totally different person."

This explains why you're always spring-cleaning your house, emptying cupboards, and clearing out the garage. You are looking for hidden bottles. You obviously don't trust him.

Listening to her story, it was easy for me to fall into the same trap: Ted's behavior could be explained by his background—a troubled kid who grew up without any moral compass and no parental guidance. Gloria was mirroring the words penned by Stephen Sondheim in *West Side Story* when the Jets say:

> Dear kindly Sergeant Krupke,
> You gotta understand: It's just our bringin 'upke
>
> That gets us out of hand.
> Our mothers all are junkies,
> Our fathers all are drunks.
> We never had the love that ev'ry child oughta have.
>
> We ain't no delinquents,
>
> We're misunderstood.
>
> Deep down inside us there is good!

My walking buddy believed that, deep down, Ted had good in him and she was determined to prove it, both to herself and to others.

But I was not prepared to do that. He was an adult now, a middle-aged adult, and he had choices. He was no longer under the influence of his family. He was his own person and did not need to be defined by his past. Besides, he had Gloria back in his life. She loved and cared for him. He did not deserve her. Why do these intelligent, independent women fall for these jerks?

Ted's court day eventually came and went. There were no headlines this time. I asked Gloria what the outcome was.

"Oh, they fined him and he has to attend AA meetings now."

I wondered who paid the fine. I knew that in the past few months, while waiting for his trial, Ted had closed his shop. His gift boutique didn't generate much business. I suspected Gloria was chipping in and helping him with finances, hoping that the shop would keep him busy and away from the bottle. Some hope!

Gloria liked to read, and I often passed on to her the books I'd read. One day when I went to her house with my latest stash of pre-owned books, I saw Ted sitting on the porch doing his woodwork. I watched as he expertly chiseled that small piece of wood. If he had any skill at all, this was it: he knew how to carve small figures out of wood. But a chill went up my spine when I saw the array of chisels and knives next to him. A man who could lose it so quickly should not have these potentially lethal tools at his disposal.

Without thinking, I said to him, "I thought you were in jail."

"They let me out," he replied, looking rather downcast and sad.

"Well, try and keep out of trouble."

"I'm trying," he said, sounding as if he meant it. He was not his usual bombastic self, and I sensed a change in him. Perhaps the thought of going to jail had sobered him up, at least temporarily. He probably sensed that this was his last chance, and I hoped the AA meetings would help him kick his addiction.

I also thought that Gloria could benefit by going to Al-Anon, and I gave her the number to call the local Al-Anon meeting place.

***

Excrement Hits The Fan

Several times, I tried asking Gloria whether she attended Al-Anon, but all I got were evasive answers. She told me that she drove Ted to his AA meetings, which was good news since I didn't think he'd have gone on his own—court orders or not.

A couple of months went by, and Christmas was approaching. The few weeks between Thanksgiving and Christmas kept me busy. I drove to Colorado to visit friends. We made a special excursion to Mesa Verde, and I came back refreshed and ready to spend Christmas at my son's house. He and his wife were hosting this year.

I told Gloria I had to put our walking on hold, and she seemed okay with it. "I still have some unpacking to do and loads of laundry. Give me a week, and I'll call you when I'm done," I said.

"No problem, call me when you're ready."

I went about my business, writing cards, putting up the Christmas decorations, and looking forward to spending time with the family. Since my husband Peter's death, my kids fussed and worried about me. I didn't want to become a burden. I hated the thought that they might be saying or thinking: "What are we going to do about Mom?" My friendship with Gloria and Myrtle meant that I had a life and was content and self-sufficient.

My Friend Gloria

I was on the stepladder trying to hang a Christmas wreath over my front porch when the phone rang. Darn! Why does someone call when I'm busy and the phone's out of reach? I tried to ignore it. It'll go to voicemail. If it's important, they'll leave a message.

As soon as I got down from the stepladder, the phone rang again. It was Gloria. I picked up, saying, "Hey, you missed me so much you can't wait…"

"The shit's hit the fan," she interrupted.

"What do you mean? What happened?"

"It's Ted. I'm at my son Mike's house. I've been here since Saturday, and today we're going to county court to take out an eviction and restraining order on him."

"Are you okay? How can I help?" I was confused, but not surprised. I had wondered how long it would be before Ted unleashed his violence on her. "What can I do to help?"

"We're leaving right now to get the restraining and eviction orders. Then Mike will take me home and change the locks. I'll call you later and explain."

Oh boy! This must be really bad, but she's finally come to her senses. Not knowing the details, I hoped she wasn't badly hurt. Deep down, I was glad things had come to a head and she'd realized that she was better off without him. She was safe with her son and she'd call me when she was ready.

Myrtle called me first. "We've had a lot of excitement here again," she said. "You missed all the fun!"

"Fun? What kind of fun?" I asked.

"The police came and escorted Ted away while Gloria's son changed the locks to her condo."

"Did he put up a fight?"

"No. He went quietly. Didn't even get a chance to pack a suitcase."

"Well, I'm glad she saw sense. Hopefully, she'll get her life back now," I said.

Both Myrtle and I agreed it was for the best that Ted was out of Gloria's life and no longer around our neighborhood. "We're all sighing with relief," Myrtle said.

Eventually, Gloria did call me to tell me that Ted had been drinking. She could smell alcohol on his breath. When she confronted him, he denied it. He became violent and threatened to kill her. He tried to push her down the stairs and hit her across the face. She locked herself in the bedroom and hid there. Finally, she managed to call her son, Mike, who picked her up. She spent the weekend with Mike, and on Monday, she got the court eviction and restraining orders.

I listened to her story in silence. I was not surprised. A man with such a short fuse and a drinking problem would eventually turn on his partner. "I'm a strong woman," she said. "I don't need a man in my life. He's a liar and a cheat."

"Well, you are now free to live your life as you want," I said. She could be whatever she wanted to be. Not wrapped up in Ted and his needs.

"We can resume our walks again," I said. "Christmas is coming soon, and I need to lose the weight I gained over Thanksgiving to make room for Christmas pudding. Will you be spending Christmas with your son this year?"

"Yes. He's a good cook."

I was glad to hear Gloria making plans to be with her son. She never said so, but I sensed that Ted had come between them and alienated him too.

We resumed our morning walks, but I was uncomfortable when she kept bringing up Ted's name in conversation. She still hasn't got him out of her system, I thought, despite her repeated statements that she was an independent woman who didn't need a man in her life.

A few days after Christmas, I asked her, "How was your time with Mike? Did he prepare a feast for you?"

"I didn't go to his place. He went hiking on Christmas Day."

"Where did you spend the day? If I'd known you were alone, you could have joined me and my family," I said.

All I got was a vague answer. She was becoming good at that, and I did not want to pry. Then Myrtle came by one morning for a cup of coffee. In her usual Myrtle way, she burst into my kitchen saying, "He never left. That son-of-a-bitch, never left!"

"Who? What are you talking about?"

"Who do you think? Ted!!! He's back, with a new car and a new set of keys to her house. Two days after she kicked him out, she let him back in again."

"I can't believe it!"

"I'm telling you, it's the honest truth. Jason's not happy either. We thought we'd gotten rid of him for good."

I was so surprised, I nearly scalded myself with the coffee. I sat down across from Myrtle and tried to think. She lied to me. All the time she pretended she was alone, she allowed him in through the back door. No wonder she did not spend Christmas with her son. He probably was so disgusted with her, he went off on his own. What a mess! That explains her evasive answers.

I felt gutted, sick to my stomach. Myrtle got up and poured the coffee. "Here," she said, "get yourself around this. It'll calm you down. You've been a good and loyal friend all this time, and she lied to you. We all feel let down."

"Are you sure?" I hoped that Myrtle was wrong, but deep down I knew she wasn't.

A couple of days after Myrtle's bombshell, I called Gloria and asked her point-blank if she was back with Ted. I tried to remain calm and not show my annoyance.

"Oh yes. We're working things out. He has to have treatment for his illness and attend CBT (Cognitive Behavioral Therapy) sessions three times a week, as well as AA meetings for his addiction. I also go to CBT for my addiction, which is Ted."

She said this matter-of-factly as if it were the most natural thing in the world. She even sounded happy to have her abuser back in her life. "Well, I hope you're safe. You know where I am, and I'll be here for you if you need me," I said and hung up.

His disease: my foot. You're nothing but his enabler. He's hit you, tried to throw you down the stairs, threatened to kill you, and you are glad to see him back? Any other woman would be glad to see the back of him. What kind of person are you?

After that, my relationship with Gloria changed. It went into refrigeration—not quite deep-freeze, but it couldn't be the same. She had lied to me, and I felt let down. I wanted her to be the strong independent woman she said she was or pretended to be.

***

It's said that pets give you unconditional love, but even a pet, when badly treated, will turn on you. Gloria remained under Ted's spell and put up with all his abuse and humiliation.

Feeling angry and frustrated, I began to analyze the reasons I had pursued this friendship. Was it a co-dependent relationship, like the one she had with Ted? Perhaps, I liked to think that she needed me—

that I was her only friend and confidante. It's probably my fault. I like to be needed and liked. It feels good to be needed and necessary. I was drained and exhausted. I had carried more than half of that relationship. In my convent school, I had been taught that sacrifice and putting others first was how I should behave. Was I trying to save Gloria from Ted and her low self-esteem, in order to feed my own need to be wanted and liked? In my efforts not to be a burden on my children and to be independent, perhaps I was looking for lame ducks who needed me.

All these thoughts floated in my head. I feared I was spiraling into depression until Myrtle came by one day and said, "Come on, I've booked us into a nail place and after our mani and pedi session, we're going to Tom and Jerry's for ice cream. Then we're going back to my place for a snack and maybe we'll watch a video… and I'm not taking 'no' for an answer."

True to her word, Myrtle picked me up, and as luck would have it, we were the only clients in the nail salon. She must have been a regular because she knew the names of the two Vietnamese assistants who greeted us with the usual "Pick cohow Mettel," which I translated as "Pick a color, Myrtle." We dutifully chose our colors—mine was a salmon pink, and Myrtle's a bright magenta. Nail salons, once you overcome the language barrier, are ideal places to relax. Your feet are in a tub with warm, swirling water, and the massage chairs recline and work on your back, while the assistant works on your feet. Ahhh! Sheer bliss!

Sitting side by side, Myrtle told me that for several years she had been volunteering at a women's refuge.

"You mean for battered women?"

"Yes. They escape from abusive relationships, fathers, husbands, boyfriends, and we take them in. Sometimes they arrive with their kids and nothing else."

"Wow. I didn't know that. How did you get involved?"

"Oh, a friend told me about it. My father abused my mom and me. He used to beat us, so I wanted to do something to help."

"That's very noble of you," I said. "Perhaps we should give Gloria the address of this place. She's going to need it sooner or later…"

"You bet. But I know from my experience at the shelter that women return to their abusers. We keep the address of the place secret, but for some reason, I can't understand why they go back. Sometimes they leave up to seven times before making that final break."

I was silent. Myrtle understood the Glorias of this world better than I did.

"I know how much time you invested in Gloria," Myrtle said. "And I know how disappointed you are. But take it from me: you can't get emotionally involved in these cases. You have to step back and let them make their own choices."

"Gloria is going to Cognitive Therapy sessions," I said.

"That's good, but it's a long-drawn-out process, and she has to keep all her appointments. I don't think she does. Sometimes I don't see her leave the house for days, and neither does Ted."

Myrtle was the tonic I needed. She brought some sense and balance into my muddled thinking over Gloria. I was able to let go of my resentment and anger. I shot an email to Gloria saying that I was there for her if she needed me, hoped she was safe, and gave her the websites and numbers of local organizations that help victims of domestic violence.

***

Gloria never tried to get in touch with me again. I felt that our connection was so damaged that it'd never recover. I didn't trust her anymore. I had closed that chapter: end of story. Or so I thought until, like a recurring nightmare, Myrtle phoned me at five o'clock one Tuesday morning: "You'd better hear it from me," she said, "before you see it in the news. Ted is dead, and they arrested Gloria."

I was speechless. Myrtle continued: "I don't have any other details, but we woke up with the police arriving and escorting her out of her home. The house is full of police. Jason went over to see what happened, but they wouldn't let him in. Once I know more, I'll let you know."

"How do you know he's dead? Did you see him?"

"Jason knows one of the officers who was there, and all he got out of him was: 'The guy's dead.' I know he shouldn't have said that, but he and Jason worked together a few years back."

She was right. Later that day, the local media reported that a man had been found dead in his house and the police were investigating. Do they suspect foul play? Do they think Gloria did it? Did he drive her to it, until she finally couldn't take it anymore? The media said that the police had a "person of interest" in custody. Is Gloria the 'person of interest'? Myrtle said that Ted's body had been removed and Gloria did not return to her house.

"She might be at her son's," I said.

"No. I saw Mike and spoke with him briefly when he came to the house. She's not with him. He looked sad, and I didn't ask him whether he knew where his mother might be. If she isn't with him, she must be the 'person of interest, 'I guess."

After several weeks, the media reported that Gloria had been arraigned and was in police custody. There was no mention of bail. Myrtle and I were convinced it was self-defense. She must have snapped and couldn't take it anymore. Self-defense most likely.

It became a cause célèbre. For the first time in my life, I knew the defendant—a rather dubious honor—in a criminal case. For this reason, I followed it closely on both public and social media. So did Myrtle. We remained convinced that it was self-defense—justifiable homicide. For years we'd seen how sad and troubled Gloria looked. We knew she had tried to get him out of her life using eviction and restraining orders, and, truth be told, we were both relieved that Ted was no longer and felt guilty at the same time.

We just wanted him to go away, not dead.

***

Finally, when we knew the date the court would reconvene for the jury's decision, Myrtle and I joined the crowd of news reporters and others who also wanted to hear the verdict. The trial had lasted several weeks, and the jury had taken another week to reach its decision.

Judge Hooper had presided over the proceedings. I thought of the Socratic definition of a good judge's duties: to listen courteously, answer wisely, consider soberly, and decide impartially. He had certainly met the first two criteria, now I was about to see how he fulfilled the last two.

Before he called in the jury, he turned and addressed us. "We are about to hear the jury's decision. I don't know what that decision is, but some of you may not be happy with the verdict. If anyone has strong feelings or thinks they are not able to contain their reaction to the jury's verdict, they must leave the courtroom now. If anyone reacts loudly or makes any noise or comment, I'll hold them in contempt and have them removed."

Wow! He didn't mince his words. He certainly wanted silence in court.

The jury came in and took their seats.

"Who is the foreperson?" Judge Hooper asked.

"I am, your honor." A woman in her mid to late thirties with light brown hair stood up.

"Have you reached a unanimous decision?"

"Yes, we have, your honor."

"Then please hand your verdict to the bailiff."

The foreperson handed the folded paper to the bailiff, who took it to the judge. Judge Hooper read it in silence. The suspense was almost audible. We all held our breath. My brain was screaming: What's the verdict? Tell us!

Judge Hooper nodded and passed it on to the clerk.

I was on tenterhooks, and my hands were clammy. I didn't dare look at Myrtle sitting next to me, but I could feel her body tremble. My legs were shaking so uncontrollably that I thought they'd take off and leave me stranded there. All eyes were now fixed on the clerk. She cleared her throat and read out loud: "In the circuit court of San Diego, we the jury find the defendant, Gloria Janssen, guilty of first-degree premeditated murder."

There it was. The rest was a blur. My head became an echo chamber with the words: "First-degree premeditated murder" bouncing around. I glanced briefly at Gloria, who stared straight ahead. I looked away as tears ran down my face. Don't make a sound, or the judge will throw you out. Is he going to sentence her now? I can't get my head around this. I think Myrtle is crying too.

Judge Hooper looked at us and said: "Before I pass sentence, I want to say a few things," and he paused to take a sip of water. The overcrowded room was hot and stuffy, but silent.

"This has been a protracted case. It has been a case of note and has taken a lot of time and energy. We're here today to hear the jury's verdict and to decide what an appropriate sentence would be in this case."

So here we go. He's going to pass sentence now.

"The court has only considered the evidence presented here. The court has accepted the jury's verdict." At which point, Hooper took another sip of water. I too needed some water. My mouth was so dry it hurt.

"As we all now know, Ted Sabatini was murdered by Gloria Janssen with several stabs to his chest from a chisel. He fell backward down the stairs, but she did not attempt to save him or call 911. Instead, according to the evidence we heard, and the pathologist's report, she waited several hours and then called her son, telling him that Sabatini had an accident."

At this point, Myrtle turned and looked at me with a big question mark on her face. So Mike knew about Ted's death! Was he in cahoots with his mom?

"The defendant wanted her son to go to her home and help her, but instead, he called the police." So it was Mike who called the cops.

My thoughts were interrupted by Judge Hooper, who said that before the trial, he had ordered a psycho-evaluation of Gloria to find out whether she was competent to stand trial. That's why it took so long. They had to do a psychological evaluation of her first.

Looking directly at Gloria, he said: "You knew that your lover, Ted Sabatini, suffered from bipolar schizophrenia and was on strong medication. You deliberately withheld his meds, plied him with drink, and caused him to have several manic episodes where he became violent. You then pretended that he was abusing you and that he was an alcoholic. When you found out that he was going to leave you and return to his family, you killed him."

In the deathly silence that followed, I felt a dark cloud hanging over me. I'm going to be sick. They should have sick bags like they have on airplanes. I wish I hadn't come. Where's the nearest exit? I wondered whether I was having a panic attack, whatever that might be. The Gloria sitting there in court was not the Gloria I knew. It wasn't the same person. I didn't want to believe that my friend was the monster that Judge Hooper was describing.

The judge's voice filled the room: "Ted Sabatini was a sick man, both physically and mentally. He suffered years of ill-treatment and abuse at the hands of the accused, Gloria Janssen."

How could I be so stupid? Blind? She fooled me, and like Ted, we all were her victims. We believed her and felt sorry for her. She played us. We too were victims of this scam artist.

No time for introspection—that could wait. The voice from the Bench continued, clear and crisp: "Therefore, Gloria Janssen, having been found guilty beyond a reasonable doubt, by a jury of your peers, of first-degree premeditated murder, I am going to sentence you to life with a mandatory minimum of 25 years in a state prison."

I think the judge also said something about Gloria having the right to appeal. I wanted to appeal, but where would I appeal and to whom? What was I guilty of? Stupidity? Naïveté? Having been conned? I wanted to wind back the tape and change the script, but I couldn't. I felt so empty, confused, and powerless. That was it?

Myrtle whispered to me: "Thank goodness it's over." I wasn't so sure. It wasn't over for me. I'm the one who's going to need a psychological evaluation.

The press were the first to rush out, then the rest of us filed out in silence. Myrtle and I were among the last to exit, both too numb to say anything. I felt that my legs were about to collapse from under me. A crowd had already gathered outside the courthouse. It was mayhem. I held onto Myrtle as we navigated past the crowd, past the press with their clicking cameras and noise. It was midday. The sun shone, but I felt darkness and I was shivering.

Myrtle gave my arm a squeeze as she led us away: "I think it's a mani/pedi day," she said, tears streaming down her face.

I nodded.

My Cousin Nick

I was an only child. My cousin Nick, a few years older, became the brother I never had. He'd cycle for miles in the burning heat of a Greek summer to bring me my favorite candy during school recess.

We were both born on the Greek island of Crete to low-income, working-class parents. Nick's family remained poor, while mine prospered and moved up from working to middle class. That was a big leap on a small island where everybody knew everyone else's business and origins. Everyone aspired to move up the social totem pole, but not all succeeded. And, if you did succeed, there was no shortage of people who'd remind you where you came from. "Don't get too big for your britches," or, "Now you think you're too high and mighty?" were phrases quickly hurled at the hapless person who dared to dream, or who attempted to rise above their birthright of poverty and lack. If you wanted to "make it," you had to look beyond the confines of your village or small island. You looked to Athens, the capital, with its cosmopolitan lifestyle, university, and theaters, where nobody reminded you "where you came from."

Nick was the son of my mom's older sister, Alexandra. She had hoped to study agronomy in Athens, but lack of funds, imagination, and low family expectations had relegated her to the role of wife, homemaker, and mother. That's what was expected from all females back then. If you remained, God forbid, unmarried or were widowed, it was considered your duty to take care of other family members—parents, kids, and the needy. "Every family needs a spinster," Mum often said. She made sure it wasn't her.

Young girls were taught the skills of homemaking—cooking, cleaning, caring for younger siblings or elderly relatives. The ultimate goal was marriage. And here too tradition prevailed—the norm being that you married within your class. The rich married the rich and the poor married the poor.

Her dreams thwarted, Alexandra poured all her hopes and ambitions into her son. She encouraged Nick from an early age to espouse more highbrow interests—classical music, dance, and the arts. She was also determined that he'd become a successful doctor, never considering that he might not be capable or even willing to embrace medicine.

Mum wasn't always happy with the way her sister raised her son. "Why do you always have him dress up and dance in front of your guests? He's a boy. Teach him to be a man."

"Oh, but he loves dancing, and he's so cute. He loves performing. He gets into his role better with the right clothes," my aunt responded.

"He should be out with the other kids, kicking a football or a can down the street."

"Hell hath no fury like a mama protecting her cubs," was another of Mum's aphorisms. My mother had plenty of those—one for every occasion. She thought her sister was being overprotective.

Alexandra paid no attention. Wanting to mold him to her own perceptions and ideas, she continued to buy for Nick books on the classics and medicine. Early on, she banned from their home the music that blared out of Greek taverns and immersed her son in the melodies of Bach, Mozart, and Puccini.

"I don't want him to grow up with that bouzouki cacophony," she said. "It's vulgar!"

Nick's father, Tony, a bit rough around the edges, had been known to be a good soccer player. The rarified atmosphere that his wife cultivated so carefully for their son alienated him from them. He retreated to the local taverna, where bouzouki music, gossip, and male locker-room talk prevailed. He had already lost the battle over the upbringing of his son.

When I was old enough to become aware of family dynamics, I asked my mother, "Why did Auntie Alexandra marry Uncle Tony?"

"It was arranged by our parents."

"Are all marriages arranged?"

"In those days, most of them were. Your Uncle Tony saw Alexandra and fell in love with her. She was beautiful. He offered to marry her without a dowry."

This was a godsend for my impoverished grandparents. Despite Alexandra's protestations, they forced her to marry him. Different times, different mores.

The year Nick graduated from high school, he and his mother flew to Athens, where she enrolled him in medical school. The metropolis she had visited as a young woman had changed, but there were still museums, theaters, and ancient sites to explore before she returned to their island. She planned to be his guide. The Acropolis was beckoning. She'd take him to the Parthenon, art galleries, and the theater.

***

For Greeks, myth and history are so intertwined that often it's difficult to separate them. We never question the existence of Jason and the Argonauts, or Daedalus and Icarus, or Pygmalion and Galathea. Were they real people? Is that story based on fact or fiction? Is the Iliad based on facts?

Instead of nursery rhymes or stories from Hans Christian Andersen, I grew up with the stories of heroes who fought in the Trojan War, the Labors of Hercules, and the shenanigans of the gods on Mount Olympus and the tricks they played on humans. The *Odyssey* was not just a book on the shelf gathering dust. The exploits of Odysseus and his travels came alive, as my father read segments to me from Homer's classic.

I recall a cruise trip with my father around the Greek islands when I was eight years old. As we passed by the island of Icaria, my father, never one to miss a chance to moralize, reminded me of the story of Daedalus and Icarus.

"Why were they flying?" I asked, eager to know more.

"They were fleeing from King Minos in Crete after Daedalus had built the labyrinth at Knossos."

"Why?" I was good with the "whys" as a child.

"Because King Minos didn't want Daedalus to share the secret of the maze. Same with the pyramids. Their builders were killed so nobody would know how to enter or exit them."

I wanted to know how they managed to escape. Dad obliged. He loved retelling the old tales of King Minos, Hercules, and the Minotaur.

"The only way they could escape the evil king was to fly away. Daedalus made wings for himself and his son Icarus. He warned Icarus not to fly too close to the sun because he used wax as glue, and the sun would melt it. That's how they escaped."

"So what happened?" I wanted to know.

"Because he didn't listen to his father, Icarus died. He flew higher and higher and closer to the sun. The wax that held his wings together melted, and he fell and died. That's what happens when you don't obey your father. You see that island we are passing now? It's called Icaria. That's the spot where Icarus fell to his death."

Most children's stories end with "And they lived happily ever after." The stories I heard ended with: "And the moral of the story is..." Aesop's legacy had been passed down to my family.

It never dawned on me to ask how a boy could become an island. My father's statements and admonitions had that ex-cathedra quality about them, and my father's warning remained. "Don't fly too high or too low. The middle road is best." We were still learning from the mistakes and examples of our ancestors, or so I was taught to believe.

My Cousin Nick

***

It was no wonder that Aunt Alexandra wanted to revisit the grandeur and glory of ancient Greece while in Athens with her son. It brought back memories of her girlhood. Nick embodied for my aunt her unattained dreams and hopes—he would succeed where she hadn't.

Alas, this time too, her plans were thwarted. A few days after they arrived in Athens, she died from a massive stroke. She never got to see her son graduate. Left alone in Athens, he mourned her passing, but he was determined to fulfill her dream. He would become a doctor.

He never returned to Crete, and I lost touch with him. Fate also plucked me out of Crete and took me to England, where I studied, grew up, and married. From time to time, I heard about Nick from my mother. One day, she called me.

"Guess what? I've got exciting news. Your cousin Nick is coming to London."

"For how long?"

"He's coming for work. He's staying with me for a while."

I looked forward to seeing him again. When we met, he was vague about his prospects. He said he needed a couple more diplomas, as well as an internship, before he could become a full-fledged doctor.

***

Once again, life intervened. We moved to Singapore with my husband's job. When we returned to London six years later, Nick was working as a doctor in various hospitals in the UK. As ever, my mother was our point of contact. Having a soft spot for him, she assumed the role of being his surrogate mum. She kept abreast of his news, his jobs, and promotions. He was a rising star in the medical world, and she was very proud of him. Every time she called, she spent half the time talking about Nick. She always said, "If only his mother could see him now. She'd be so proud of him." I agreed with her. It was a cruel blow of fate that Aunt Alexandra died so young, and never got to see her son become a doctor.

Any time one of us had an ailment, even a simple cold, Mum would say: "Wait, don't do anything until I ask Nick." She trusted the doctor in the family—just because he was family—more than any other doctor in the UK's National Health Service.

"But Mum, our local surgery is only down the road. Nick is a hundred miles away in the north of England!" I'd say.

"So what! He's family, and he knows. I'll call and ask him. It never hurts to have a second opinion."

At times, her adulation of Nick and his ability to cure all our ailments was irksome. And not only to me. Any chance she got, she'd mention him. Standing in line to pay for groceries, waiting for the bus, even in her own doctor's surgery, she'd strike up a conversation and, never missing a beat, brag about her nephew, the doctor, the rising star in the field of orthopedics. Whenever I referred to him as the 'Bone Doctor,' she'd object: "Why do you call him that? He's an orthopedic surgeon. Say it properly!"

"But Mum, it's only a joke. Everyone knows what that means."

"You're belittling his credentials. Don't put him down."

There was no point arguing. She was as stubborn as her late sister. I sensed that her hypersensitivity about my cousin was based on guilt. She had broken away from the preconceptions of our island. When Alexandra died, she did not step up to take care of him as was expected of her. She did not offer to contribute to his education or have him live with her. By the time Alexandra died, Mum was divorced from my father and busy traveling overseas in search of a second husband. She'd never admit it, but I knew that a heavy load of regrets and self-reproach lay festering under her obsession with her nephew's career successes. Her break with tradition came with a ton of guilt.

**

My Cousin Nick

When my mom died, Nick came to her funeral. When my marriage died, he was also there, supporting and helping me. But whenever I reminded him of our childhood in Crete, he'd cut me short: "I don't want to hear about Crete. I'm an Athenian now. That's how I think of myself. My heart and soul belong to Athens. Crete means nothing to me."

"But don't you want to visit? Go back and see family and friends for old times 'sake?"

"No! Crete means nothing to me. What is Crete? Full of ignoramuses."

"Really? Crete gave birth to the Minoan civilization, one of the most advanced in antiquity," I reminded him. But to no avail. With one grand gesture, he populated our island with half-wits.

"I don't care. I don't want to talk about it." He'd say this with so much venom it was a closed subject. He was fixated on Athens and the mainland. He had definitely inherited the stubborn gene that plagued our family.

As a hospital doctor, he worked long hours, but whenever he had time off, he'd call, visit, or arrange for us to go to some cultural event. He'd appear on my doorstep with tickets for the opera, a concert, or an art show. He was indeed a 'culture-vulture'. His mother's subliminal messages from the cradle up had taken deep root. My tastes were more eclectic, which at times led to arguments. He did not approve of my liking jazz and ABBA or having an interest in other cultures.

"It's jazz. I love traditional jazz. Listen to the rhythm. It's Benny Goodman."

"Goodman, mooshman. How can you stand that noise? Play some Bach. I've got tickets for the entire Mozart season at the Barbican in London."

He made similar disparaging comments about anything that failed to meet his criteria for aesthetics and refined taste, from foreign food to the purveyors of those delicious Indian curries and sweet and sour Chinese dishes. I tended to overlook his peculiarities—his dilettante ways and snobbery—because he was always kind to me. We shared a love for classical music, the opera, and travel.

He was keen on foreign travel. I once commented on the many suitcases that accompanied him. "Why so much baggage when you're traveling solo?"

"Well, I need a change of clothes. I'm not one of those peasants who wash their socks in the washbasin of their hotel room."

"But you carry too much weight. You must pay for excess baggage each time."

"So what? I need to have casual wear for the day when sightseeing, then change into something more formal for the evening. And for dinner, I change into a tux. I need the shoes and shirts that go with each occasion and each suit."

"But you're a tourist, for heaven's sake. Why go formal in the evenings? You're not a guest at Buckingham Palace."

"I like to dress for the occasion. I don't know how to travel 'light, 'as you put it."

"What's wrong with jeans and a couple of T-shirts?"

"That's for workmen. I don't dress like that."

He was certainly a dandy dresser. His wardrobe was filled to the brim with expensive cashmere sweaters, several pairs of leather shoes, and expensive suits. He cultivated good taste to extremes. To me, he oozed with pretense.

However, there was one character flaw of his which I found deeply offensive. Whenever we were out together, he always spoke to me in Greek, making rude and derogatory comments about the people around us. Total strangers drew his fiery darts about the way they dressed, walked, talked, looked, or behaved. He'd pick a target and start: "See that woman who just crossed the street? She's dressed like a maid. I bet she's one of those refugees from an uncivilized country. How dare she walk into Selfridges? They should show her the door."

"How is she supposed to be dressed, according to your dress code?"

He missed my sarcasm. He was on a roll. "Going into a prestigious shop like that, you should dress accordingly. Her shoes are filthy, and her hair's a mess. She must be a whore. Look at all that makeup! On that ugly face! Disgusting!"

His constant finger-pointing was an addiction. He just could not stop. I recall one occasion when we were at the Royal Festival Hall in London. As we sat outside in the forecourt waiting for the concert to start, another theater-goer joined us. London being a big, overcrowded city, it's common to share tables with strangers. Right on cue, Nick turned to me and started his diatribe in Greek. "Look at him. Look at his face. He hasn't shaved for days."

"Does it matter? What difference does it make?"

"He's so unkempt. He looks like someone down from the country."

I looked at the man. There was nothing peculiar, unclean, or unkempt about him. He wore a nice tweed jacket and tan pants. I made some neutral comments. For the next twenty minutes, while we waited for the concert to start, I had to listen to my cousin's toxic torrent of verbiage about this poor man. When it was time to enter the hall, our belittled and maligned companion turned round and said to us, "Enjoy the concert," in perfect Greek. Nick's face went crimson.

I hoped the incident would cure him of this nasty habit. But no! The embarrassment was short-lived. Each time we met, he was the same. His diatribes were downright rude and disrespectful. It was useless trying to divert his attention or get him to stop. It was an obsession. He needed to put down everyone else because that was the only way he got his self-worth. From time to time, I'd call him out on his criticism and name-calling. I'd remind him of our poor antecedents and the fact that our grandmother was illiterate. He'd get upset, and we'd have an argument.

After each row, I'd ignore his phone calls, until he'd turn up on my doorstep with an expensive bouquet of flowers and tickets to a concert or art show. I felt sorry for him because I sensed I was his only "friend." He sometimes mentioned various colleagues, but I never met any of them. As far as I knew, no one ever visited him. He was lonely but would never admit it.

He retired early because he had a minor stroke. I went to help him settle back into his apartment when he was discharged from the hospital. The place was crammed with "stuff." He had a considerable collection of shopping bags, many from various supermarkets. I tried to throw away several stacks and he went ballistic. "What are you doing?" he exploded.

"I'm throwing them away. You have about thirty here. You only need a few."

"Don't touch them. I need them!" he shouted.

I was surprised by this rather over-the-top reaction. I then discovered the real reason behind the stack of shopping bags. Whenever he went to the neighborhood shops and discount stores—and there were quite a few in his neighborhood—he'd place his bagged goods inside the bags from the more prestigious shops and department stores. He'd sail in front of his neighbors and the concierge with bags that boldly announced their high-class provenance: Harrods, Harvey Nichols, and Selfridges. He wanted to impress and show off that he shopped at these expensive stores. The local thrift and discount shops were beneath him. He craved affirmation and admiration, going to extremes to get it. He maintained that he was popular and loved by his colleagues and all the staff who worked at his apartment complex.

"They love me. When they need a reference or an application to get their kids into college, they ask for my help."

"Well, I guess when you sign off as a medical doctor, it carries more weight," I said.

"Last Christmas, I invited them into my apartment and treated them to caviar and smoked salmon."

"You did what?" Was this a joke?

"Yes. I invited the concierge, janitor, and porters to my place and offered them caviar and smoked salmon."

"You forgot the oysters and foie gras," I said tongue-in-cheek—my sarcasm going unnoticed. He said he wanted to "educate" them about the "good things in life," and show kindness. Nothing but showing off. You're a condescending buffoon.

He worked hard at trying to show off and impress. This was his opium and it was poisoning him. I couldn't understand why a doctor constantly needed to belittle others. A therapist would have a field day with him. I often thought of saying, "Hey Nick. You need to see somebody and get cured of your pompous and asinine ideas."

My Cousin Nick

Egomania and superiority complex are addictions and hard to cure. There's no Al-Anon or AA equivalent for them. Nick would never condescend to stand amid strangers and admit: "I'm a megalomaniac and I need help." He'd take one look at those present, judge them to be inferior, and walk out. Narcissism is an incurable disease.

***

You can't choose your family, goes the adage. I could not change him, but he did have some redeeming qualities. Nick was there for me during some difficult times in my life. He felt he was my protector. He'd often say: "You know, I'll always be there for you. You're my little sister." It was ironic that however hard he tried to appear cosmopolitan and urbane, he reverted to the role of protector and provider assigned to males in our culture.

He was knowledgeable about classical music. He often brought the music score or librettos to the concerts. He couldn't read music, but he could pretend.

He was also a pack rat. Whenever I visited him, I could hardly move around his apartment without bumping into piles of magazines and papers stacked on every surface and even the floor. "Why do you have all these old magazines and promotions for luxury hotels?" I'd ask.

"Because I have subscriptions to them. I can stay there whenever I want."

The few times I tried to tidy up, he got agitated and cross.

"You changed my station. Now I can't find Classic FM on my radio."

"It's about time you connected to other stations too. I must have turned the knob when I dusted your radio," I replied, realizing that he was totally inept at finding the station by himself. I had to find it for him. He couldn't even change a light bulb.

My cousin was a total technophobe. He never learned to use the internet or a simple cell phone. I even bought him one and spent time showing him how to use it. He kept it on his kitchen countertop and never charged it. "I have no interest in this new-fangled technology," he'd say—the usual excuse given by those unable to master it.

"I hate computers! I loathe them," he kept saying.

"If you had your way, we'd still be traveling on donkeys, like our grandparents. You're a Neanderthal," I'd reply. "You can never go back to work without computer skills."

"Not at all. I'm a scientist. I have a medical degree and am well-informed on all things medical. I don't need a computer to tell me how to do my job. I prefer to examine the patient. Lay my hands on them and not rely on a machine to tell me what's wrong," he said. He preferred the old-fashioned ways of doctoring. And to some extent, I sympathized.

He always had a beautifully arranged bowl of fruit on his table. On one occasion, I said, "How about having some fruit? I fancy the pomegranate."

"I don't know how to cut it," was his response.

"What! You always have them in your fruit bowl."

"Yes. I wash and polish them with a soft cloth. Don't you like the way they look? They shine atop the apples and other fruit. They're beautiful."

"So... if you don't eat them, what do you do with them?"

"I like to look at them. I rub some olive oil over them, just as I do with my dyed Easter eggs. They're so pretty."

"And when the pomegranates go bad?"

"I throw them away."

I realized that the fruit was there for looks only. The same with alcohol—the same half-dozen unopened bottles sat year after year atop his elegant showcase, gathering dust. "Nick, don't you ever drink your booze?" I asked.

"I don't drink. I buy them from the duty-free shop when I travel."

"But you've had them for years. What's the point if you don't drink?"

"I just like having them, and if I have guests, I can offer them a drink."

"You're more likely to poison them. Those bottles have been sitting there forever. The wine has probably turned into vinegar by now."

"Well, I'm a doctor. I can always cure them."

Nick was unquestionably an aesthete. He needed to have beautiful things around him. He oozed an aura of cultivated good taste. Whenever I showed concern at the cost of some of the items, his response was always: "I'm lucky to have a doctor's pension. This affords me the luxuries I want and need."

I had no response to that. He lived in a make-believe bubble of his own making, where he felt comfortable and refused to consider another reality. I sometimes wished I had a little pin to burst that delusional balloon. But what would that achieve? He was happy living his fantasy. Don't many of us create scenarios or live a reality of our own making to avoid facing up to something unpleasant or painful? I call it a delusional justification. Or delusional reality. My perceived reality is different from yours. My circuitry is unique to me. I may share some of it with others, as Ancestry.com keeps telling me in its indefatigable efforts to find my kith and kin—but I cherish that uniqueness. It's a paradox that while we beat the drum of diversity, we freeze out those who don't vote, or look, or behave like us. We preach diversity on our terms. Nick did not believe in diversity. To him, everyone was inferior, with a few exceptions. I was one of them.

***

A couple of years after my divorce, I decided to take the plunge and try internet dating. No need to tell Nick. I knew he'd disapprove, as indeed he did when I introduced him to Charles, aka Chuck. Chuck was an American from New Mexico. After several months of exchanging emails and phone calls, he came to visit me in London. We had a great deal in common, and when he asked me to marry him, I accepted.

My family was dubious about my going to live in the US, but the strongest objections came from Nick. He was adamant I was making a mistake.

"Where on earth is New Mexico? Why are you going to Mexico?"

"It's not in Mexico, it's part of the United States."

"Never heard of it. It must be one of those backward states, full of ignoramuses."

That seemed to be his favorite word. Even our birthplace, the island of Crete, was full of them, according to him. I don't know how he'd react if I'd dated someone from Crete.

"Well, I like him, and we're getting married. So get used to it."

"But America. Why America? Why can't you live in a civilized place like London? America is full of guns and murderers. They shoot kids. It's not safe. And what kind of name is Chuck?"

"It's short for Charles. And what does a name matter, anyway?" I replied.

He insisted on pointing out all the negative news about the US. For him, London was the most civilized and cultured city in the world, next to Athens. Of course, some of this opposition to Chuck was the fact that he'd lose his theater-going companion—me. I knew by then that once he got an idea into his head, nothing could change it. He was as stubborn as a mule. I once said that to him: "You're stubborn like the mules from our island. They won't budge once they decide they'll stay put. You're like them." He was furious.

"How dare you insult me like that?"

"Because you are stubborn. You're so inflexible in your beliefs and prejudices, you remind me of our mules."

To calm his objections about Chuck, I said: "You know, even Shakespeare mentioned the word 'chuck 'in *Lady Macbeth*." He was incredulous until I showed him the quote. From then on, he insisted on calling Chuck "Charles." "Chuck" was too common for him.

Chuck and I married and settled in New Mexico. Contrary to Nick's dire warnings, New Mexico was not the Wild West and certainly not full of ignoramuses. He visited us a couple of times, and I could see a gradual softening of his dislike of all things American. But the snobbery remained: "You should have settled in New York or San Francisco—more civilized than here. At least New York is only a five-hour flight to Europe."

"I like it here," I said.

"How can you like this place? There's no culture. You lived in the midst of theaters, museums, and concert halls in London. They say

My Cousin Nick

New Mexico is a high desert. It's worse than that, it's a cultural desert. How can you like this?"

He felt I had come down in the world.

He remained an arrogant dilettante and refused to admit that his ailments and slowing down were due to the aging process. In his later years, his body failed him. He suffered from gout, and this restricted his movements. He became a recluse and relied on the porters and cleaners at his condo to run errands and to shop for him. I wondered whether he was still treating them to smoked salmon and caviar. Since he had no internet and didn't know how to use a cell phone, I called him on his landline from time to time. I could hear the deterioration in both his body and mind, although he always insisted he was "fine."

***

A few years later came the sudden and unexpected news of his death. I was his next of kin and also the executor of his will. I had no choice but to fly to London and sort out his affairs. I dreaded the thought, knowing what a hoarder he was. It was a mammoth task, tiring and tiresome. Death had come upon him suddenly, and he had not prepared for it.

His closets were full of expensive clothes, many with holes because the moths had feasted on them. As for the stacks of papers in every nook and cranny, many had silverfish crawling over them. I found a vast supply of cans of food, stashed in cupboards, stored inside the oven, the washing machine, and under the tables. Many items were several years past their expiration dates.

Most of his stuff ended up in the dumpster. What was usable went to the Salvation Army. I left his desk and personal papers for last. I felt I was invading his personal sanctum. I opened his desk with some reluctance. I wanted to find a list of his colleagues to inform them of his passing. I needed to find his address book ASAP. I was grieving and tired.

My search yielded something unexpected. Suddenly I was overwhelmed with a gamut of emotions—anger, disappointment, and disbelief. It can't be! Nick, how could you do this? Who are you?

I was devastated. I discovered numerous rejection slips and failed reports which proved that Nick had never graduated from medical school. My cousin was a fraud. I looked up the register of UK surgeons and Googled his name with the dates and hospitals where he said he'd worked. There was no mention of him. No wonder he hated the internet. His lie could be exposed with a single click.

I was reeling from shock. How could he do this? Who was he? His whole life was a sham. Was our relationship a sham too? Was his interest in me, his affection and caring, part of the carefully orchestrated persona he had so carefully cultivated? All those years he had pretended to work as a surgeon in various top hospitals, was a lie. Was I just a peg on which he hung his fantasy? Was the posturing and pretense just a cover-up? Or did he really believe his lies? He had lived a fantasy—and sucked us all into it, the way a spider draws its victims into its web. This was a carefully constructed maze of lies, illusions, and delusions.

I couldn't wrap my head around it. I had tolerated his intolerance and affectation because I felt I owed him my loyalty. He had shown me kindness when I needed it. Was that a sham too? I was angry and confused. How could he have deceived us like that? How could we have been so naive, so stupid? I felt betrayed, cheated.

His last job was in a small provincial hospital in the county of Essex, east of London. I called the hospital, and they confirmed that Nick Papadopoulos had worked there for seven years as a patient care assistant—the new-fangled name for a hospital orderly. They said he was one of their best workers, always working overtime and doing double shifts. Of course. That's how he could afford to splash out on expensive clothes, theater tickets, and holidays.

I mourned the loss of a cousin, alongside the tarnishing of memories––of all the things we had shared. I felt duped and taken for a ride by a con man. The young cousin who cycled in all weathers to bring me my favorite candy was a charlatan. From now on, all my memories of our times together would be tarnished with anger. How was I to remember him? As a charlatan? A caring and loving cousin? There was such a disconnect between the two now. Perhaps with time, I could find a way to reconcile them.

The little boy who had been nurtured to become a doctor by his doting mother had spent a lifetime living her dream and fooling us—all the way to the grave.

Musings in D Minor
Givers and Takers

Vicky exploded: "I can't take it anymore. I've reached the end of my tether."

I met her through a support group for caregivers, and this was a typical *cri de cœur* from most of us. I had been caring for my brother, Jack, for over a year and realized that I, too, needed support. I got tired of hearing from well-meaning friends: "Make sure you take care of yourself," and similar pearls of wisdom. I wanted to scream back: "How can I take care of myself when I'm too tired to eat, clean my home, or even remember to take my meds!"

Exhausted, I was reminded of a book title I once saw: "Where Do Mothers Go To Resign?" Except I'd have changed that to "Where Do Caregivers Go To Resign?"

That's when I joined a support group for caregivers.

"A support for carers?" asked Charis, my granddaughter. "Why do carers need a support group? I thought that's what they like doing, to care."

"Well, honey, it's not that simple. Sometimes caregivers get tired, also. Often caring is forced on them. They care not by choice, but by necessity."

69

"Nothing is ever simple," she sighed with the wisdom of a fourteen-year-old.

At fourteen, Charis was questioning everything and everyone. Highly intelligent and curious, she was interested in what was going on around her. She was the apple of my eye, and I enjoyed our discussions, even our disagreements. Unfortunately, she and her parents lived three thousand miles away in Massachusetts, and I was in San Diego. I was grateful to her for reaching out and encouraging me to use Zoom, FaceTime, and WhatsApp. I joined the technological age because of her. Every time I contacted my son via Skype or Zoom, she'd take over, both parents withdrew, leaving us to chat as long as we wanted. She was the best tonic for me.

***

Until my brother arrived on the scene fifteen years later, I was an only child. My mother said I was a daydreamer. I had my secret place where I'd go to meditate, cogitate, and tell my problems to the surrounding trees and birds. A space behind the garden shed, overgrown and neglected, became my special refuge, away from my parents 'squabbling and shouting. It felt good to be there alone with my thoughts.

Years later, having survived adulthood, marriage, and widowhood, I was reluctantly thrust into the role of caregiver for Jack. He was fifteen years my junior, never married, and did not have any friends. A loner and not socially adept, he never invested in a retirement fund and lived on Social Security after retiring. Over the years he had drifted from job to job. Jack was always the one who was let go. "You mean you got the sack?" I told him one day.

"No. I was let off," he responded in his usual curt way.

"Why was it always you who was let go and not the others?"

"Because they could replace me with younger and less expensive people."

There was some truth in that, but I also knew that many of his colleagues and contemporaries had kept their jobs. He was always the odd man out. He preferred his own company. Being an *oops baby*, he was indulged by my parents. I suspected that he was planned in an effort to keep their marriage together. To me, it felt as if he was merely the *bandaid* over the cracks. Now, I was left to pick up the pieces of what remained of his sad and lonely life. You'd think with our age difference, he'd be the one taking care of me, should the need arise. But it wasn't to be. He couldn't even take care of himself. He was good at one thing—laying guilt trips on me and whining. He was a germaphobe and avoided physical contact as much as possible. Even shaking hands was a problem for him. Loners and hypochondriacs make good companions. Hypochondriacs are good at manipulating and controlling those around them.

As time went on and the burdens increased, it got me thinking about life in general, and how the world seems to be divided into givers and takers. Nowadays, there was no secret place behind the shed where I could go and think. I couldn't turn the clock back, but I could reach deep into my memory shed, filled with a lifetime of experiences and knowledge.

My friend Terry is one of the nicest, kindest people I know—always welcoming, hospitable, and willing to help others. One day she said, "I know I shouldn't feel like this, but I'm fed up with people who always have time to accept my invitations, whether it's for a cup of coffee or dinner, but never have time to invite me back. They're takers!"

"And I know you're a giver," I said. "Do you feel they're taking advantage of you?"

"Sometimes….yes. You know me. I love people and like to be around my group of friends, but since Stephen died, they all offered to come and visit, not one thought of asking me out. I don't expect much, but a cup of coffee would be nice. Just to sit and talk, some other place than my home."

I could see her point and to some extent, I empathized, since I too had experienced the same thing—having been the recipient of takers ' selfishness and thoughtlessness. They always had an excuse: I'm not a good cook like you, or, My house is not as nice as yours, which meant my house is dirty, messy, untidy, etc., which basically came down to the same thing: I can't be bothered, but I'll accept your generous hospitality any time. They always had time for that. I wanted to say, "There's always the little coffee shop around the corner if you think your house is not up to your perceived standard of perfection."

Terry, like me, has concluded that there are two kinds of people: the givers and the takers. Givers are those selfless souls who rush to help, succor, and support their fellow humans. Takers are those at the receiving end, always needy, demanding, and taking. Of course, this is a gross generalization, but, like most generalizations, it has more than a grain of truth in it. If there were no givers, there'd be no takers, and if there were no takers, there'd be no givers. Givers, most of them in my experience, are not good at taking or receiving. It's not in their DNA. Whether consciously or subconsciously, they follow the adage: it's more blessed to give than to receive. They even find it hard to receive compliments. A shrink would call this a co-dependent relationship. Wikipedia defines co-dependency as "… a controversial concept for a dysfunctional helping relationship where one person supports or enables another person's addiction, poor mental health, immaturity, irresponsibility, or under-achievement."

I tried to explain this to Charis saying, "Givers give because they like to give. It gives them a sense of well-being, goodness, and purpose. The takers are the needy with a victim mentality. They enjoy their misery and neediness. They're also selfish and demanding."

"Well, Granny, I know which one you are," she said.

I hoped she saw me as a giver. Lately, I started reading the *Dear Abby* column in our local newspaper. After the crossword and Sudoku, this has become a daily practice for me. A great many of the letters and requests for 'advice 'come from people who have a relationship problem. It usually concerns a dysfunctional friendship between a taker and a giver. Takers rarely write to *Dear Abby*. It's the givers who do. The writers complain about a taker who has become a drain on their time, money, and goodwill. Time and again, Abby will tell them that this type of relationship is not good for them. She gives them tips on how to break away and engage in more healthy friendships and hobbies. I wonder whether they ever heed her advice.

From time to time, a person at the receiving end of a giver—a taker––will also write to *Dear Abby* asking for help. These are the "victims" of givers—givers who use their giving as a means to control and manipulate. This got me thinking about the real motives behind the giving—it may not always be altruism. Perhaps givers need to be loved, appreciated, respected, and feel that the only way they can achieve this is by giving.

Human relationships are complex because humans are complex beings. How we navigate obstacles, trials, and successes depends on our DNA, alongside our life experiences—nature and nurture. In the final count, we alone are responsible for steering our ship through life. I know this is stating the obvious, but it brings us back to the subject of givers and takers. It appears that this generation is dealing with a double whammy of takers. More and more graduates can't find jobs. Young people suddenly develop panic attacks, depression, and other issues that prevent them from entering the workforce. They need help in many areas—physical, mental, and financial.

Looking back with the benefit of hindsight, those millennials and Generation X parents, who hovered over their offspring and helicoptered them around, enabled them to become entitled and self-absorbed. They are now reaping the results.

According to CNBC (Consumer News and Business Channel), youth suicide rates rose 62% from 2007 to 2021. It can't all be blamed on COVID-19, neither is the problem confined to the US. It's a global issue. Mental health is a big problem for Generation Z. They feel let down. One of them said to me: "I bought the lie that hard work, a good education, and a good job would give me a comfortable life, fulfillment, and happiness. It's a pipe dream. I can't afford to buy a house close to my place of work. I can't leave my job because, with a sick wife, I need their health coverage. I feel trapped and frustrated. Is this the American dream? It's a nightmare."

"How do your parents feel about your situation?" I asked him.

"They expect me to take care of them. They said having made sacrifices to raise me well and send me to college, it's now my turn to look after them."

This is something I heard many times from Gen Z-ers. I call it the treadmill of unfulfilled expectations. The givers expect to be repaid for their giving, and the takers feel trapped and unable to respond. We used to call it the generation gap. It is now an unbridgeable chasm.

Therapists and psychologists are doing a roaring trade. Parents, concerned about the mental state of their children, go to them for help. They refer their kids to experts, hoping that a cure or solution will be found for their children's malaise. The sessions are long and protracted. These specialists charge by the hour, so the longer the sessions last, the more money they rake in. It may sound cynical—some conditions genuinely require time—but when it comes to mental health, in most cases a cure is elusive.

Wouldn't it be better if we paid these therapists, and all doctors for that matter, at the completion of their treatment? I love to envision a day when we pay our doctors while we're fit and healthy and stop paying them when they start treating us. And, if the condition is incurable, they'll have to tell us and stop treating us. Who knows? This might be the case down the road, in ten or twenty years. That would balance the seesaw, as opposed to the current divvying of pills and other meds for the slightest complaint. I am not referring to cancer or dialysis treatments and other justified and effective interventions. But there's no denying the fact that the current opioid crisis is due to doctors overprescribing painkillers and other meds. In the give-and-take world, the medical people would take our money to keep us healthy.

Recently, a new law called "The Sunshine Act & the Open Payments Program" aims to increase transparency about financial relationships between healthcare providers and pharmaceutical companies. This is one of many efforts made to keep that teeter-totter on an even keel.

Transparency and honesty create integrity in most human transactions.

Of course, not all children are ungrateful brats or suffer from mental illness or emotional instability. Many do care for their elderly parents and look after them. This is something I learned from my caregivers' group. Caring for my brother Jack had put me in touch with people who are in similar situations. Amongst the many benefits of a support group is that we can share openly and not pretend. I realized that resenting my brother and the imposition he put on me was not unique to me. My fellow carers felt the same. And like me, they too were caught in the vicious cycle of guilt, resentment, and stress. By sharing our problems, we encouraged each other. We tried to find coping strategies and exchanged useful information.

Hearing their stories, I felt I had it easy. There was one lady who was caring for both parents—a blind and incontinent father and a physically handicapped mother. She would not consider placing them in an assisted living home. She said: "Mom and Dad were great parents and good people, I can't dump them in a nursing home. Besides, I can't afford it. My insurance won't cover it."

I could feel her pain and fatigue. The same with Vicky. She often burst into tears when describing the problems she had with her demented and aggressive mother.

"You know, I never had a good relationship with her," she said. "She was always demanding and a poor role model. I envied my friends who had caring, loving moms, who baked for them, and who were kind to me."

"Was there a father in the picture?" I asked her during one of our sessions.

"No. I never knew my dad. Mom had a succession of boyfriends, but they were never 'Dad 'to me. I left home as soon as I could. I was lucky to find a good job, put myself through college, and never looked back."

"But you're back now. What happened?"

"The social services found me. A social worker contacted me saying that my mom was ill and they were worried. Was I interested in getting in touch? They said it might help her since she often talked about me. They said they didn't know how long she had to live."

That was the "hook" that got Vicky, the giver, to get back with her mother and ended up becoming her full-time caregiver. That was two years ago. Vicky's story reminded me of some of the letters I read in the *Dear Abby* column: absentee fathers or mothers turning up and expecting their children, the very children they'd abandoned, to take care of them. Or children who leave the nest after causing heartache and havoc and turn up years later to claim their "inheritance" when they learn of a parent's passing.

Outsiders, like *Dear Abby*, not directly involved, come up with clear-cut solutions to these situations. But for the individuals concerned, once feelings of guilt and shame are thrown into the emotional cauldron of stress, indecision, anger, and remorse, it starts to boil over—difficult to step back and make a cold, calm, calculated decision. That was Vicky's situation. After putting up with her mother's ingratitude, tirades, and abuse, she had no choice but to place her in a nursing home that catered to people with dementia.

Vicky, however, continued to be burdened with guilt. She kept asking herself, and the group, whether she had done the right thing by her mother. We kept telling her she'd done her best, but each week it was the same story. Vicky would end up in tears when she recalled her mother's latest outburst. We don't know what happened in the intervening years, but Vicky had changed. She'd mellowed, but the mother hadn't. In some cases, the roles can change, but the norm is that givers remain givers and takers continue to demand and take.

***

The US lags behind developed countries in health care, family benefits, and unemployment support for its people. There's no national welfare safety net. It is not the remit of this story to dwell on these shortcomings. Suffice it to say that they create inequality and feelings of anxiety and fear. To some extent, it may explain the lack of respect and trust for the government.

I recall how surprised I was when, at a dinner party, we were discussing the new rule regarding white LED lightbulbs replacing the old incandescent ones. An elderly man sitting next to me exclaimed:

"The government doesn't tell me what to do!" I laughed because that was the most asinine comment I'd heard in months. I wanted to ask him whether he used his car seatbelt or stopped at a red light while driving. That's exactly what governments do—we vote them into positions of power to run the country, make laws, and govern us. If we all took and acted on that rebellious attitude, lawlessness would reign.

The lack of a national welfare system may explain the large number of charities, GoFundMe appeals, self-help, and support groups that exist in the United States. My inbox is daily heaving under the weight of "begging letters" and petitions for money for several causes. Some are very worthy and noble. Medicare and Medicaid help to some extent, but not everyone is eligible or able to tap into them. And we have entities that want to do away with Medicaid and Medicare. They argue that people on welfare are takers, lazy, and undeserving.

Exhausted and depleted from numerous overseas military engagements, the US has neglected the needs of its citizenry and the upkeep of its infrastructure. This neglect has been exposed by the nation's ill-preparedness and inability to deal effectively with a spate of wildfires, floods, hurricanes, and tornadoes—just to name a few. Entire communities were devastated and thousands made homeless. Most household insurances do not cover flooding. Often there's a clause in many policies that states that the policy does not cover "natural disasters." Floods, wildfires, and mold are often exempt from cover. When it comes to the crunch, insurance companies are good at quoting the "small print" in order to avoid paying. This is now increasingly the case. Some insurance companies refuse to insure homes in flood-susceptible areas. The same goes for wildfires. Medical insurance companies have been known to remove coverage for someone with a long-term illness that requires expensive, long-term treatments. Who are the givers and who are the takers in this instance? Should we regard insurance companies as "takers"?

We seem to trundle along happily until something like a major catastrophe exposes years of neglect, indifference, and corruption. Damage from these natural disasters could be minimized if infrastructures had been maintained and preventive measures taken before they happened. It's common sense. Common sense, however, has become a rare commodity, and in some instances, has disappeared. The victims of these disasters, who applied to FEMA and other local agencies for help, are not "takers." They are entitled to compensation and help, and that goes for the majority who are on Medicaid and Medicare. In a democratic country, it is the duty, and one of the primary roles of the State to take care of all its citizens, especially the poor and underprivileged.

I'd be the first to admit that a national welfare system can also lead to abuse. Years ago, in London, I worked on a government program aimed at getting the long-term unemployed back into the workforce. Unemployed people drawing benefits were told that their benefits would be withheld unless they attended our one-week course. This was the state's effort to reduce the number of people on the dole—the takers—and help them get back into the workforce. They came unwillingly, angry, and some even threatened us. I remember one 16-year-old girl declaring: "They can't make me go to work." I didn't say anything. "If they force me, I'll have another fu#*ing kid. They can't make me, and I ain't going," she said.

"How many do you have?" I asked.

"I got one."

"You said your mother and your grandmother are on the dole. Couldn't they look after your child while you work?"

"Nope. And they can't make me get a job, neither."

She was adamant. It was obvious that being on the dole was a multi-generational way of life in that family. Those were her role models. She triggered my interest. After she'd calmed down, a couple of days later, I got to chat with her. Both her mom and grandmother had been teen mothers. Both got pregnant under age. She too. Fathers were local youths who soon vanished. They were mere sperm donors but never took responsibility or cared for their women or kids. Givers? She was a taker by nature and nurture. However, these three generations of women stood by their kids and raised them. They cared for them and were their providers. They parented them as best as they could. Unlike the fathers, they did not abandon them. When this girl spoke about her child, I noticed a certain softening in her voice. She cared. She was one of thousands of takers—refusing to work and expecting the government and taxpayers, like myself, to keep her in the style she'd become accustomed to. But at the same time, she believed that she was the only one who could and should take care of her child. She took from the state so that she could give to her kid.

This symbiosis between givers and takers exists throughout the world, including the animal kingdom. With animals, however, the taking and giving is usually short term—limited to infancy and early childhood. The kids are shown how to fly, hunt, and survive on their own. If only we'd learn from their example. I don't know whether lion cubs, eaglets, or calves suffer from panic attacks or depression, but once they reach maturity, and are given the tools and shown how to survive on their own, they are launched into their surroundings to fend for themselves. Some species remain in groups or packs, such as wolves, monkeys, and dolphins, but they are part of the group and are expected to survive on their own if the need arises. Of course, there's a pecking order, even with birds and animals, and the fittest survive. Nature does not molly-coddle.

With humans, however, because we are at the top of the pyramid, survival becomes more complicated. When faced with the realities of life, some of us, especially the young, often become fearful and depressed, develop anxieties, and are unable to cope. Many resort to suicide. Navigating the human jungle requires a hybrid mix of education and knowledge, as well as a frequent topping up of life experiences—the good and the bad.

The distinction between the giver and taker gets somewhat blurred here. Like most things in life, it is not always a matter of black or white. By indulging their kids, enabler parents derive a certain satisfaction. They see their children as a conduit for their own ambitions and unattained goals. Parents of child prodigies often live vicariously through the success and achievements of their children. Having high expectations for your kids is fine. But not breaking the umbilical cord and not giving them the tools to become independent, self-sufficient, and useful members of society is poor parenting. They fail their children and society at large and create a generation of drones—takers who lead parasitic lives. They haven't learned reciprocity. If there's no balance between giving and taking, between the individual and the common good, we'll have anarchy and lose the high moral ground we boast of—the rights and privileges of free speech, freedom of assembly, free press, and a peaceful transition of power after an election.

To a great extent, social media has contributed to the malaise and stress we experience today. Daily broadcasts, podcasts, blogs, and vlogs, be it digital, printed, or televised, elicit feelings of anxiety, envy, anger, and curiosity. Many people use social media to show off to their loyal followers and "friends," which they often count in the hundreds. They crave recognition and praise in the form of "like" ticks and comments of approval. Even the most inane "oohs" and "aahs" satisfy their egos. They give out information to get a reaction. This craving for affirmation has made them addicted to validation. One media content entrepreneur, Katy Steckly, admitted as much on her many channels. Social media has become ego masseurs and masseuses to many.

Added to this mix, we now have a proliferation of so-called influencers. These are people involved in marketing. They sell an idea, a service, or a product, and we buy. Social media has become a marketing platform. Give and take. No harm done. But when social media creates in their users feelings of inadequacy, fear, FOMO (fear of missing out), or envy, we have to take a step back and examine the motives of both givers and receivers. Social media has become a playground for narcissists and manipulators.

The negative effect of social media has been well documented. According to 2024 data, the average daily usage of social media is 2 hours and 23 minutes. According to the Pew Research Center, 69% of adults and 81% of teens in the United States use social media. This puts a large amount of the population at an increased risk of feeling anxious, depressed, or ill as a result of their overuse of social media. Too much time is spent hunched over the cellphone or computer, scanning, searching, and isolated. Ironically, something that's meant to bring us together seems to isolate us from one another.

***

Giving and taking is something we encounter every day in life, from the personal and particular to the general. The interaction between the two is like a seesaw—a fine balancing act. If there's an overload on one end, the subtle balance is lost, and problems ensue. This is particularly evident in international relations and government interactions. For any administration to govern effectively, there has to be a certain give and take—from the bottom up and from the top down. A good government has to listen to its people. This is true of any democracy.

Democracy can be messy because it needs input and participation from many to achieve the common good. Interestingly, the Greek philosopher Plato called democracy mob rule. He promoted the idea of government led by philosopher kings—what today we'd call "aristocracy." Nowadays we have meritocracy—rule by those who deserve to govern—or so we believe to be the case. The US is ruled, for the most part, by a plutocracy because of the vast amounts of money needed to mount a campaign and remain in power.

Political power is held by those who survive the grueling marathon of running for office every four years or so. It's a perpetual treadmill of demand and supply. Give and take. Candidates come cap in hand seeking a handout from us—money and votes—promising to give us, once they're elected, something in return. Powerful pressure groups with vested interests become generous donors and funders of wannabe politicians. They give, expecting to receive in due time. It's give and take: You scratch my back and I'll scratch yours.

Not all politicians are liars or con artists, but when in office, they're faced with new situations and realities. Once elected, officials cannot fulfill every single promise they made while campaigning. However, they remain beholden to their largest donors. The balance tilts in favor of their big and powerful sponsors, leaving the rest of us stranded. They bow to the interests and demands of those who shelled out thousands and millions to get them elected.

Gun violence is one prime example of this imbalance. The figures are appalling. According to NIHCM (National Institute for Health Care Management), over 42,000 people died as a result of gun injuries in the U.S. in 2023. The number of people killed by firearm violence, a leading cause of premature death, grew by nearly 43% between 2010 and 2020. Children continue to get murdered in their classrooms by criminals. It's a no-brainer to see that Congress is impotent to enact strict gun control laws because of the massive donations and influence of the NRA.

In recent years, we've seen even Supreme Court justices being jetted and feted by billionaires who lavish on them expensive gifts in the form of holidays, private jet trips, and paying their kids 'school fees. The separation of powers that was once the hallmark of American democracy has now disappeared into the infamous cesspool of corruption and shamelessness.

Big corporations do the same. They take care of their shareholders first while looking for loopholes to avoid paying their fair share of taxes. Many have their head offices in offshore countries, such as the Cayman Islands, where they pay no taxes. Their actions increase their profits but add to our tax burden. Any shortfall is made up from our tax contributions. It's the same when shops are forced to pass their losses from shoplifting onto their customers.

The rich take care of the rich because they benefit each other. One such example is the Trump administration's reducing taxes for big corporations and wealthy donors. Where does that leave the rest of us? We gave them something very precious—our vote and/or money. But the widow's mite does not count and is not valued in the kingdom of greedy, powerful corporations and leaders. We unwittingly become their enablers. Again, these are exceptional cases. Some corporations and officials perform well and are effective.

**

Apart from personal feelings of guilt, humans can also suffer from societal and historical guilt. Collective memory and written archives bring forth and expose periods of darkness—wars, genocide, and prejudices such as racism and xenophobia. In most enlightened cultures, we see efforts made to address these wrongs and make amends. The intentions are good and necessary, but the results are often dubious and messy. One such example is the Brown v Board of Education Supreme Court decision in 1954. It eventually led to desegregation in schools, but at the time, busing caused riots and pain to the children, who were used as the first guinea pigs in this attempt at social engineering. Being polarized is not conducive to good results, however well-meaning.

Positive discrimination was another well-intentioned effort that backfired. Giving as a result of guilt does not necessarily have beneficial or positive results. Positive discrimination prioritizes a protected characteristic over merit and qualifications, potentially disadvantaging others and jeopardizing the principle of fair and equal opportunity. By leaning towards 'favoring 'and enabling one section of the population, it discriminated against another. It remained a highly contentious subject in US education, and in 2023 the Supreme Court ruled that race can no longer be considered a factor in university admissions. The ruling upends decades-old US policies on so-called affirmative action.

Today in the United States and Western Europe, these endeavors are made in the name of diversity. Diversity is an umbrella word for efforts made to address prevailing abuses and discrimination. Results, however, remain mixed, and not always successful. Hate speech, gender, and race discrimination are outlawed. However, social, economic, and gender injustice remain. The aphorism: "The road to hell is paved with good intentions" is befitting in this instance. That does not mean that we shouldn't try and make this a better world, but awareness and a deep understanding of the human psyche, along with empathy and common sense need to be deployed.

Change takes time, and time is something we're running out of. Every generation has had its dark and difficult moments, but today we live in the nuclear age, the climate crisis age, the rise in the crazy dictators-with-nuclear-weapons age. Thanks to the digital age, news travels fast—bad or scary news travels even faster. We have a heightened awareness of these dangers. The need for drastic change is more imperative than ever.

***

Musings in D Minor can be monotonous because it's always in the same key. I needed to add other notes to my piece. This is where my small group of friends came in handy. They are my family by choice. We met through a local Tai Chi class and over the years, we cemented our friendship by sharing, commiserating, and celebrating together. We met once a week at some local eatery or coffee shop and sorted out the world's problems. Even if we didn't have an answer to ours, we certainly had solutions to the problems besetting the universe. We had diversity in shape, size, age, and color. We called ourselves The Thinkers Think Tank (TTT). I can't remember who came up with that name, but it was a good fit.

I was glad to have them in my life. I was aware that I used them to vent and complain about my brother Jack and was monopolizing their time. But I also felt that they were there for me, and as their situations were different from mine, it gave me a welcome relief from my "Jack problem." Ken was our token male, in his sixties, and very wise and knowledgeable. Fran was the pragmatist. Suzy was the joker who saw the funny side of most things and made us laugh—witty and bubbly. Mary was an attorney, and anything relating to legal matters was addressed to her. And then there was yours truly, the one with the "Jack problem."

Lately, our conversations centered around the very subject of givers and takers. When I mentioned how animals let their young go as soon as they are ready, Ken said: "You know, not all animals abandon their young. Some stay together in packs or herds, such as wolves and elephants."

"That's how we get the saying 'Birds of a feather flock together, 'just like us," said Suzy. That made us all laugh.

"When we talk about givers and takers," Mary said, "humans are hard-wired to have empathy and the need to help others. Not everyone is self-centered or selfish."

"Yes, but those are the givers," I said. "If, as you say, we're all hard-wired to help and feel empathy, how do you account for the narcissists and takers?" That started a whole new debate. There was a good balance of different views, and if we agreed to disagree, that was fine too. The different viewpoints were what I loved about us. The discussions were lively and stimulating.

Ken turned around and asked me, "Melissa, you've lived in China and traveled a lot, do you think that people in other countries are different from us?"

"In my experience, I think most humans, the world over, have basic needs and want the same things—safety, a roof over their heads, food on the table, and a future for their children. How they go about it varies, but they have the same hopes and aspirations as the rest of us," I said.

Mary chipped in, "Taking the theme of giving and taking a step further, there is now a global concern among many countries, including China, Japan, Italy, the US, and India—to name just a few——that have a low birth rate and an aging population problem."

That was my cue. "China is facing a tsunami of consequences from its one-child policy. It succeeded in limiting its population, but now they don't have enough young people to take care of the old folks. For the most part, Chinese elderly are expected to remain in their family homes and be cared for by their children or grandchildren."

Fran said that in many countries, there's a stigma associated with placing parents or older family members in nursing homes. I agreed, saying, "Confucian ethics and Buddhist tradition place the responsibility of caring for the elderly on the children. It comes under the guise of 'filial piety, 'and there are many stories that reinforce and praise this tradition—a tradition that goes back thousands of years."

"We don't think like that in this country," sighed Fran.

"When I lived in China, young people often asked me, 'Why are you here? 'And I'd reply, 'To earn money so that I can eat. 'Invariably, their reaction would be: 'Why aren't your children taking care of you? 'They believe that since parents raise children, it is the children's responsibility to show their filial piety and care for their parents when they get old. That's the harmony between yin and yang—give and take. Today, the new economic prosperity and better quality of life are not conducive to procreation."

Mary said, "Young people are more career-minded and females are not eager to return to the traditional roles of feeders, breeders, and carers. Ergo, the low birth rate—the yin and yang are out of synch there. They call it 'progress.'"

We all agreed that women now had freedoms and privileges their mothers didn't have. But did this mean we had created a better world?

"By jettisoning some of our age-old traditions, I think we've lost something of our souls. And we are also faced with the same question, 'Who is going to take care of the elderly in the future?'" Mary said. "I worry about this myself. I have no children. Who is going to take care of me?"

That day, our TTT meeting had a somber note. It gave us food for thought because most of us were either retired or close to retiring. I got engrossed in the discussion and was glad I did not bring up my Jack problem.

***

In the past few years, there's been an increase in articles, podcasts, websites, and social media concerned with the same problem, "Who is going to take care of the elderly? Can the country afford it? Is Medicare going to run out?" A recent headline in the *San Diego*

Union-Tribune read, "San Diego's senior population to increase in the coming years, raising concerns for elder orphans." We have an increase in the number of elderly, and the tone of the article was alarmist and sensational, stating: "In the next 10 years, adults over 65 will outnumber children under 18 for the first time in United States history, according to Census Bureau data. San Diego County's senior population is projected to grow by more than 21% in that time. Also growing is concern about a group known as elder orphans—people who don't have the support of spouses, children, or close family."

This question is echoed in the chambers of Congress, AARP, and elsewhere. However, no solutions or plans have been put in place. In the meantime, the clock is ticking. In a free-money or capitalist economy, money will buy you care, including euthanasia, which is now increasingly available in the United States. It's called the End of Life option. In the past, people with money traveled to countries that offered physician-assisted suicide. Those without the funds, or who did not believe in euthanasia, become the "elderly orphans." I wonder whether in the future, "End of Life" options will no longer be an option but mandatory. I recalled Aldous Huxley's book *Brave New World.* A shiver went up my spine and became a thought: Are we beginning to live for real the fantasies of nineteenth and twentieth-century sci-fi writers?

***

Going from the ridiculous to the sublime, we should not forget the genuine philanthropists and charity organizations who give generously without ulterior motives, such as Doctors Without Borders, Mercy Ships, and Help No Kid Hungry. Alongside these, we should also add the many self-sacrificing souls who devote or have devoted, their lives to helping others. In particular, Mother Teresa of Calcutta and Malala of Afghanistan. Not ignoring the thousand acts of kindness that do not attract attention, such as a neighbor turning up with some home-baked cookies, a church organizing a meal rota for someone who's unwell, or a stranger helping you lift that heavy Home Depot sack of soil into your trunk.

In democracies, when we have cases of injustice, poverty, racism, and marginalization, we have advocates such as the ACLU and private individuals who take up the cudgels to advocate for these causes. They give their time, voice, and energy, and are prepared to suffer ridicule and even imprisonment in some cases. They give to a cause they believe in. They help those who cannot help themselves.

Like most actions, giving and taking have ripple effects. Whatever the motives or reasons, we must keep that teeter-totter on an even keel. The pivot is the Golden Mean, and in a perfect world, it should be horizontal. The greater the instability surrounding us, the more the seesaw becomes unbalanced and teeters up and down in response to situations that throw us off balance: the downturn in the economy, rumors and threats of war, mass shootings, weak ineffective administrations controlled by vested interests—the list is endless.

There's no shortage of bad news aided and abetted by the adage: If it bleeds, it leads.

The first two decades of the twenty-first century have given us information overload. It's a daily bombardment—the text messages that arrive and require immediate responses, the emails that demand attention ASAP. Our cellphones have become our lifeline, and we have difficulty detaching ourselves from them. Technology has us wrapped around its little finger. It's a trap from which we cannot easily escape. Hence the frantic panic when we realize our cellphones are missing or the network is down. We've become passive recipients—takers—of what's on offer from our preferred sources.

I'm tired of being the unwilling eavesdropper on other people's cellphone conversations or having my inbox jammed with unsolicited emails. It's like Hydra's head; the moment I block one email, another five pop up. I can't even read my newspaper online without a dozen ads interrupting and competing for my attention. A friend of mine had a mantra he used as soon as he answered his phone: "If you're selling, we're not buying. If you're buying, we're not selling. State your name, rank, and serial number or buzz off." Rude, perhaps, but I empathize with his frustration. He later became an Anglican vicar. I suspect he answers the phone differently these days.

Another factor that has contributed to the world's general malaise is that today's young people belong to the internet-raised generation. They have non-stop internet access, at least in most parts of the world with internet facilities. This too has side effects. Are we becoming desensitized to death and other tragedies? This overload of tragic news and information can easily turn us from givers to passive takers of tragic news. Apathy and indifference breed their own problems. They fester in the background until they come to bite us. One such example is mass migration caused by wars and the climate crisis. We know and are aware of mass migration movements and their effect. But once the waves of humanity head for our borders, our apathy is overturned by the reality facing us. It's now our problem. It's knocking on our door. Our apathy does not turn into sympathy or empathy—the most common reaction is that of NIMBYism—Not In My Back Yard. This particular seesaw imbalance affects all of us.

***

I discussed the NIMBY effect with my TTT friends. Brainstorming is always helpful, and my friends were good at that.

"You know the term NIMBY started back in the '70s," Ken said. "I remember the protests against the siting of nuclear plants, wind turbines, and telephone poles."

"Me too," interjected Suzy. "I was very much a Green Party supporter and advocated for wind energy until I saw how ugly and noisy those huge turbines could be. Who wants them in their backyard?"

"What has that to do with givers and takers?" I said.

"Well... we get back to that seesaw of yours. We want, support, and advocate for something until we realize it's going to affect us in a negative way. I'm all for low-cost housing, but I don't want those apartments built behind me. They'll block my view of the mountains," Fran, the realist, said. "So, as we change our minds and seesaw from one side to the other, your symbolic seesaw is affected. Up and down."

"Does that mean we give our support to various causes but take it back when it doesn't suit us?" I said.

"Exactly!" they all chorused.

"We can be givers one moment and takers the next, for the same cause. It's human nature," said Ken.

"That's life," sighed Fran. "It is what it is."

"I think it's incumbent on each of us to try and keep that seesaw on an even keel," Ken added. "We don't realize how lucky we are to live in this country. I count my blessings and I'm grateful that I can walk, talk, and think freely in a country that, although not perfect, enables me to be who I am and to have hope."

He was right. We were aware that millions of others do not have that freedom. They live under corrupt, rapacious regimes who take and take, and only give misery and pain to those they govern.

Fran said, "My brother-in-law works for the Pew Research Center. He believes that one can find data that proves or disproves any point of view, from the most extreme conspiracy theories to the most ridiculous statements. He said statistics can be manipulated to prove your truth. AI is now increasingly used for this."

That was my cue to pipe in: "You know, 'Alternative facts 'was a phrase used in 2017 by Kellyanne Conway, during a *Meet the Press* interview, trying to defend Sean Spicer's false statement about the attendance numbers at Trump's inauguration. It was a lie, of course, but the naive and gullible believed it."

"Yes," Fran added, "We've become takers and believers of mis- and disinformation because we're too lazy to do our own research, and I'm one of them sometimes. Who's got time to go and research everything that's put out there by the media or the government?"

That gave us food for thought and created a somber mood—how to separate the truth from the lies.

Suzy summed it up nicely, saying: "We must keep that questioning spirit alive and always search for the truth. The menu is vast and complicated, but we must educate ourselves to study it carefully and choose that which will tip the teeter-totter to the higher ground, for the common good."

"There's one ray of hope. Not all young people are desensitized or indifferent to the mess we and previous generations made. They know they will have to deal with it," I said.

Ken added, "That's true. Look how the efforts of Greta Thunberg and Malala Yousafzai are gaining momentum throughout the world. The campuses are buzzing with young voices calling for peace and an end to wars and violence. They refuse to be silenced or intimidated."

"Well, there's hope there," Fran sighed. We all nodded in agreement.

"By the way, why do you call it 'Musings in D Minor?'" Mary asked.

"I was hoping someone would ask me that…" but before I had time to answer, Fran burst in:

"It's considered the 'sad 'key. It started with an 18th-century composer, Christian Schubart, who said: 'Every fear, every hesitation of the shuddering heart, breathes out of D minor. 'And he spent 10 years in jail because he criticized the society of his day in his writings."

Ken pointed at me and laughed: "Well, at least you won't be jailed."

"It all depends on who our next President will be," said Suzy. Nobody laughed this time. D Minor prevailed.

***

I awoke to my phone ringing. Blast! The one time I decide to have an early night, and someone calls me… I pick up. It's my son, and before I have time to say anything, he says: "Hi Mum. I hope I didn't wake you up. Charis wants to talk to you. She needs to tell you something."

Charis needs to tell me something at 9 pm my time, while it's midnight on the East Coast? I'm wide awake.

"Hi, Granny." I know she's crying as her voice breaks up with sobs. After a few minutes, I get the gist of what she's trying to tell me. One of her school friends committed suicide. She's grief-stricken, angry, confused—the whole gamut of emotions when someone close to you takes their own life. At her age, trying to rationalize, analyze, and come to terms with the fact is twice as hard. We spend a while talking—she, trying to tell me how she feels and wondering why her friend killed himself, and me trying to find the right words to explain the inexplicable and also to comfort her.

Actions have ripple effects. Recently, a friend, who had been ill for several years, went for the California "End of Life" option. He even named the date and time and told some of his friends. I was one of them. Those of us who knew him went into shock. Shock because of the total helplessness we felt, and maybe because it also reminded us of our own mortality. His was the last act where he could show that he was in charge: both a taker and a giver. He took the one option over which he had control.

I wonder whether my brother Jack might consider the "end of life" option.

As Fran would say, "That's life. It is what it is."

Hari

I boarded the flight to China with some trepidation. As soon as the overhead light went out, I unbuckled my seatbelt and pushed back my seat. I was exhausted, but my mind was still in fast-track mode. Like the whirling blades of a helicopter, it refused to slow down. We—my brain and I—had been on overload for the past few weeks and now seemed unable to downshift. Sleep would have to take second place to the thoughts buzzing around in my head. The same thoughts I'd been dealing with before leaving England—my home, my friends, and a way of life I knew and enjoyed.

As I embarked on this new adventure, I wondered whether I was brave or foolhardy. I did not know anyone in Cathay, did not speak Mandarin, and my few words of Cantonese would be useless in Beijing. The only thing I knew was how to use chopsticks and teach English—that is what was taking me to China—not my expertise with chopsticks—but my ability to teach English.

The previous year, on July 13, 2001, China learned that it had won its bid to host the Summer Olympics. A country with a labor force of 1.2 billion people went headlong into preparations for the great event at a feverish pitch. After years of internal turmoil, feudal wars, and humiliating treaties, China was now emerging from its silk cocoon. Cathay wanted to show that it was now a world player.

Anticipating the arrival of thousands of visitors for the Olympic Games, the Communist government mandated that all Chinese working in the hospitality business, including taxi drivers, barkeepers, restaurant waiters, and tourist guides, had to learn English. When the Chinese government issues a diktat, everyone obeys. China opened its doors to "foreign experts" to facilitate this process. I was one of them.

The PRC's (People's Republic of China) need for teachers came at the right time for me. Recently widowed, I needed a change and was looking for ways to pay off my late husband's debts. With a heavy mortgage and no regular work, my financial situation was dire. Beijing came to the rescue. I had the skills, experience, and qualifications they needed. Financially, it made sense. It was also an opportunity for me to get to know firsthand this great country, its people, and its culture. If things didn't work out, I had a return ticket.

The flight was at least twelve hours long with a brief layover in Frankfurt. Fatigue eventually won, and I was able to nap for an hour. I was woken by my fellow traveler who wanted to get past me on his way to the bathroom.

When he returned to his seat, my companion introduced himself. His name was Ludwig (as in Beethoven), and he came with a heavy German accent.

"Is Beijing your final destination?" I asked. "Or are you going on further afield from there?"

"I'm getting off in Beijing. I'm going to vork there, to tich English."

"Oh, so am I. What a coincidence—we're going to do the same type of work and we find ourselves on the same flight and sitting together." This will help time pass quickly, but that accent! Way too heavy.

"Is anyone meeting you at the airport?" I asked.

"No."

"So which company hired you? And where will you be teaching?"

"No company. I'm going to look ven I get there. I don't like cities. I'll go to the countryside."

I marveled at his nonchalant attitude. "Do they need English teachers in the countryside also?"

"Oh, yah," he said, "they need English teachers effereevare."

You'd better learn to teach your students to say "yes" and not "yah." I kept my thoughts to myself.

"You know, von me it's an adventoor... Vee learned in school about the 'Yellow Peril' and vot voot happen ven the 'dragon avakes.' Vell, she's avake now and I vant to see it," he said this matter-of-factly.

I winced at the words "Yellow Peril" and wondered whether he realized the metaphor was loaded with prejudice—depicting Asian peoples as an existential threat to the West. It reminded me of those gross cartoons depicting Japanese men with exaggerated facial characteristics, as they were sent to internment camps during WWII.

With one swift brush of the pen, men, women, and children were considered "enemy aliens," and put away. The US interned most of them, but so did the UK, Australia, and New Zealand. I hoped Ludwig would refrain from using that expression while in China.

Like him, I too was looking forward to this new chapter in my life, but perhaps more cautiously. Between meals, walking up and down the aisle, trips to the bathroom, and intermittent naps, we continued our chit-chat. It helped pass the long hours of flight. I also realized that having a representative from my company stationed in Beijing and a job lined up was a bonus. When we landed, I wished him good luck and we went our separate ways. I never saw him again. But maybe, somewhere in some part of China, there are Chinese students who speak English with a heavy German accent.

I soon settled into my new apartment and job. Most of my colleagues were graduates from British universities, but I was the only one with teaching qualifications and experience. The manager of my English Language School gave me his most important clients. I found myself teaching English to Beijing's budding billionaires and CEOs. These clients had opulent offices in high-rise buildings in the business district. They brokered multi-million-dollar deals, mostly with the US. They had a basic knowledge of English but were aware of their limitations and wanted to improve. Apart from the language, I taught them how to make presentations, how to deal with clients 'complaints, to look over contracts carefully, and question everything they did not understand.

Hari

When it comes to doing business in China, the rules of engagement are different from ours. It is customary to invite the foreigner out for a meal. Usually, this will be at an expensive restaurant with something like twelve to fifteen courses. The food just keeps on coming. It's a banquet and very expensive for the host—where you talk about anything and everything except business and politics. During this time, you become *pan-yo*, which is the Chinese word for friend. After the banquet and a few more drinks—this can continue for several days—you meet in their office and draw up the contract.

My clients were part of the new China—self-assured, successful, and astute businessmen. They were not going to be browbeaten by rude and pushy foreigners. I remembered the words of my German traveling companion: the dragon was indeed *awake*.

***

Two of my clients were brothers who had visited the US many times and had extensive dealings with their Texas counterparts. Their English was good, and I enjoyed the views of Beijing from their 28-story penthouse office. After a two-hour lesson one afternoon, they asked if I wanted to work for them full-time.

"You can be our tutor and advisor. We'll pay you more, and you can have your own driver."

I was both surprised and flattered. I didn't know what to say. I thanked them and said I would think about it. I felt some loyalty to the company that had hired me in London. I shared the news with a few of my colleagues and my manager, who said, "I'm not surprised. You have all the skills they need. This is typical of them. I understand they want you to work exclusively for them. We cannot match their offer." He was willing to let me go. That was good of him. I offered to reimburse the company for my airfare if I accepted the offer.

Other colleagues, however, were not so sure it was a good idea for me to accept the brothers 'offer. They cautioned me to think twice before changing jobs.

"You know, the Chinese are harsh taskmasters," they warned. "Look at the way they work their own people. They expect 24/7 availability, and once they become your paymasters, they own you."

It was true. Years ago, when I lived in Hong Kong, I heard it said: "Never work for a Chinese company. They'll work you to death!" On the other hand, I needed the money to pay off my mortgage and debts. That was the main reason I went overseas. I could work hard, but I also needed a private life and time to myself. I wanted to travel and see more of China. I was undecided, trying to weigh the pros and cons.

Then my colleague Elaine said, "Why don't you become an IELTS examiner? The money's good and you get to travel all over China. I can lend you the money if you want."

"What's IELTS?" I said. "I've never heard of it."

"It's an English exam developed by Cambridge University. It stands for International English Language Testing System—IELTS for short. It's an international standardized test of English language proficiency. The British Council runs it. We need more examiners, and I thought of you."

"Why is the British Council doing exams? I thought it's the cultural arm of the British embassy, so why is it involved?"

"When the Chinese apply to go overseas for work or study in an English-speaking country, they need a visa. Before they can get it, they have to show proficiency in English. That's where the IELTS test comes in. If they fail the exam—no visa."

"How long's the training? I like the idea of free travel in China at the embassy's expense."

I politely thanked my two clients, declined their offer, and began training to become an IELTS examiner. The training itself was an eye-opener into another aspect of Chinese education. Our instructor was a no-nonsense Australian named Wanda. She made sure we understood what the exam entailed and its importance. A great deal of the training involved warnings about the many ways students would try to cheat.

"In today's China," Wanda said, "success is everything. For them, it's okay to cheat your way to get what you want. To them, plagiarizing is not cheating. They learn by rote and then regurgitate what they've memorized. That's their system. For that reason, most of our exams are multiple choice."

As a student, I always hated multiple-choice exams, but as an examiner, they made my life easier. Wanda also warned us that we were not allowed to socialize with the candidates or accept invitations or gifts from them.

"Most find the oral test the hardest. Last week I caught a student who had a wire carefully hidden under long hair and glasses. He was in touch with someone from outside, and I bet it wasn't for the football scores!" Wanda said.

Gosh, do we have to frisk them like airport police?

"Most of your students will be males because of the one-child policy," she said.

I was aware of this policy. Tradition and local culture favored the male child.

Over the years as an IELTS examiner, a couple of students tried to bribe me. One with a pot of homemade jam—a special regional delicacy that her mother had made—and another begged me to pass him because he needed that visa to join his sister at Columbia University.

"How come you have a sister under the one-child policy?" I asked.

"I'm from Xinjiang province," he replied. "I'm Uighur." A reminder that China's ethnic minorities were exempt from the one-child policy.

***

Hari

The exams were usually conducted regionally. Friday afternoon, the Council would fly us to a provincial center and put us up in a five-star hotel until Sunday. It was difficult to pass on those sumptuous breakfast spreads, so I had to watch my weight. Occasionally I'd sneak out a Danish pastry or some fruit for my mid-morning break. On Fridays, from 8:30 a.m. to 4:30 p.m., we carried out exams, both oral and written. The test papers came sealed in an envelope, which we opened a few minutes before the tests started. The written papers were taken back to the British Council office in Beijing, where we'd mark them later that week.

Even when I didn't have exam papers to mark, I enjoyed going to the British Council's offices. There was free tea and coffee, and stacks of English magazines and newspapers from the UK, Australia, and the US. It was peaceful and quiet, blocking out the noise of Beijing. I considered it my private club.

It was there that I met Hari. I was marking scripts, head down when I heard someone say:

"Hi! You must be the new examiner."

I looked up to a pair of hazel eyes looking at me from across the table.

"I'm Hari," she said, "short for Hariklia. My parents were Greek."

"Mine too. What a coincidence," I said. "Do you speak Greek?"

"Of course! What kind of a Greek would I be if I didn't? Let's go to the coffee room. I'll treat you to coffee," Hari said. "My treat!"

We both laughed because the coffee was free, but that was the beginning of a beautiful friendship.

***

The expat lifestyle can be rewarding and seductive. The low cost of living affords the expatriate a higher standard and a better life than in his home country. I worked two jobs in China. I earned good money and traveled frequently to other cities. My apartment complex in the Chaoyang district had a gym, pool, hair salon, and massage parlor— luxuries I enjoyed regularly. Something I could hardly afford in London.

Many of my colleagues were fresh out of college and much younger. They gravitated towards the noisy bars, pizza parlors, and franchises such as McDonald's and Starbucks—that were spreading like measles all over China. Hari was the one exception. Apart from being the same age, we were both widowed and coincidentally, she had owned a house in the same part of London, which she sold before coming to China. Her only daughter was married and lived in New York City.

"The house got too much for me," she confessed. "Since I no longer needed four bedrooms, I decided to sell. My late husband was a party animal and we did a lot of entertaining, but when he passed away— and as I grew older—it became a chore," she said.

I teased her, "When we're both done with this Oriental safari and retire, you can share my place in London. We'll be two old crocs reminiscing about the good ol' days in China!"

"Not so fast. I'm in no rush to become an ol 'fart. I still have a lot of memories to collect here," she said, laughing. "By the way, have you heard of the CCC?"

"No, what's that?"

"It's the China Culture Club. A young couple runs it, and they organize wonderful trips—both in town and in other parts of China—for expats. They speak fluent English and act as guides."

"It sounds interesting. You haven't wasted much time since you got here. What made you choose China in the first place?"

"When Jim died five years ago, I tried to settle into the new normal. My daughter lived in New York City and I thought I might try and move there. I visited but didn't like it. Why exchange London for New York? I was undecided and felt unsettled without Jim—we'd been married 37 years. Then I heard China needed English teachers, and here I am."

"So tell me about the CCC," I said.

"It's run by Feng, who says he started it on his own. They have great talks, classes, and workshops ranging from Confucius to Kung Fu, from cookery to Chinese brush painting, mahjong—you name it, they have it."

"It sounds like my cup of tea," I said. "You also mentioned trips. Are they local?"

"They have trips to all parts of China, as well as local. I've been on a few with them. Why don't you join? This weekend they're organizing a walk through the Hutong areas."

"You've got a two-year head start on me," I said. "What's Hutong?"

"They are the fast-disappearing narrow lanes of Old Beijing. They began in the Yuan dynasty, and that's where the traditional multi-generational courtyard houses—*siheyuan*—are."

"I've always wanted to visit those residences. I've read about them."

Hari went on to explain: "The Hutong are one of the most interesting parts of this city, and the government is busy demolishing them and replacing them with skyscrapers."

I had been there only a couple of months and was already accustomed to the incessant vibrating drone of jackhammers. She joked, saying, "Take a good look at that bridge or building—tomorrow there'll be a high-rise in its place." Something of an exaggeration, but the speed of "progress" was deafening.

"It's a shame they're destroying their patrimony," I said.

"On the one hand, they're proud of their heritage and boast about their six-thousand-year-old history, and at the same time, they are busy destroying it. All those ancient buildings and traditional houses are fast disappearing under the bulldozers. Beijing is losing its soul."

Hari was right. The destruction of the old to replace it with something new was not unique to China, but the speed and ruthless way it was carried out was both impressive and frightening. There were no tree-huggers or protesters to delay the process.

"That's why I joined the CCC. English-speaking Chinese enthusiasts give us insights on all aspects of their culture and traditions," Hari continued. "Last week I enjoyed a hands-on class on how to make dumplings—and how to steam them in bamboo baskets lined with lotus leaves and stack them on top of each other," Hari said.

"Okay, okay. You convinced me. Count me in," I said.

"Just one word," she warned. "Never mention the 1989 Democracy Movement or the Tiananmen Square massacre. Although Feng maintains they are not a government agency, the tentacles of Big Brother are everywhere. Just be careful."

"Thanks for the tip," I said and took her warning to heart.

Much as we enjoyed the good life and observed with awe the speed and efforts China was making to leap from feudalism and from the ravages of Mao's Cultural Revolution to the 21st century, we were not naive. Mao's successor, Deng Xiaoping, told the people that *To be rich is glorious*—but I was also aware that the Communist government kept a close watch over us. Autocrats don't brook dissent.

"Before I left England, I told my friends and family not to mention politics or religion in their emails or phone calls."

"I did the same," I said. "Great minds think alike! I'm here to pay off my mortgage, not to get arrested or kicked out."

The CCC was exactly what I needed. Through them, I visited many parts of the country and learned a great deal more than any book could provide. We visited the Tibetan Plateau, rode Bactrian camels in the Gobi Desert of Inner Mongolia, roamed around the petrified forest of Kunming, and walked along the cobblestone streets of the canal cities of the southeast. We saw silk made from cocoons in the factories of Suzhou. Our guides spoke good English, and their enthusiasm and pride in their country were palpable. No encyclopedia or guidebook could match them.

Hari was right. We were making memories. With each experience, I kept thinking, *This one is the best*, or *This is the most amazing place I've ever visited.* Until the next one, and the next, and the next.

***

Christmas was approaching, and I was expecting my friend Toby to visit from Los Angeles. Hari suggested we use my apartment to celebrate.

"You have an oven and space. Let me get the turkey, and we can invite some of our colleagues as well as Chinese friends."

Having an oven was a bonus. Traditional Chinese cooking is done in a steamer or stir-fried in a wok—ovens are not necessary.

I agreed, "Okay. Let's do a traditional English Christmas with stuffing, potatoes, and the works. We'll invite everyone."

Hari

Toby arrived a few days before Christmas Day and helped decorate my apartment in red, white, and green. She and Hari did most of the shopping and came laden with food, drink, and small gifts for our guests.

"Hey guys," I said. "What's all this? Too much!"

"It's Christmas," Hari said. "We want to celebrate in style and show our friends how it's done back home. After all, they show off their country and traditions. Let's reciprocate."

She was right, and it was great fun. We had about twelve guests, most of them Chinese friends. The stuffed turkey was the *pièce de résistance*. I'll never forget the expression on their faces when I brought it into the dining room on a big platter. Agape, they could hardly believe their eyes. They'd never seen such a big bird before. One of them asked, "What kind of animal is that?" I teased them, saying Toby had smuggled it in her carry-on from LA. Then I fessed up.

"I was worried when you told me you were going to China solo," Toby said. "But you've settled in very well. Hari's a good friend, and the CCC provides you with a lot of entertainment. You're both culture vultures. Their programs are perfect for you."

"It's true. We have similar interests. Most of our other colleagues are much younger and like to party when not at work."

Toby's visit was brief but memorable. Hari and I took her around Beijing sightseeing.

"Why is Toby always diving into an Internet cafe?" Hari asked. The internet connection in my apartment was unreliable. Computers and laptops were not as common as they are now. Internet cafes provided web access for an hour or two for a small fee. Whenever we were out, Toby was always disappearing into them. We were both curious as to the reason Toby needed to connect to the internet.

"I don't know," I said. "Why don't we ask her?"

When we did, Toby told us that she was on Match.com and was dating a couple of guys.

"You mean you're dating two men at the same time?"

"I like them both. They are different, but as I couldn't decide which one to pick, I went for both. Of course, they each think they're the only one I'm dating. They're not aware I'm dating two guys. Eventually, I guess I'll have to decide—especially if we are to meet. But for now, it's just these two."

Hari and I were surprised. To me, it sounded a bit like cheating.

"You should try it too," Toby said to us. "I've met some interesting guys online. There's plenty of fish out there. You just have to go online and cast your nets. Nothing ventured, nothing gained."

***

Hari

Toby's visit planted a seed that we would soon have to either cultivate or remove. Hari broached the subject first:

"What do you think of Toby's idea of internet dating?"

"I'm not sure," I said. "She's clearly excited about it and seems to be enjoying it. But I don't know about dating two guys at once. I'm not comfortable with that. I don't think I want to embark on some virtual adventure at this stage in my life."

Hari agreed. "I've been out of the dating game too long. I wouldn't know where to start. After Jim died, a friend of his tried to date me. It was too soon."

I wasn't interested in embarking on online dating. I was happy with my life. In a year, I'd be able to pay off my mortgage. My bank balance looked good, and I enjoyed a good standard of living. Dating would be a complication. I said as much to Hari.

"I hear you," she said. "Life is good for now. But I'm not getting any younger, and I do miss not having a male companion to share my life with."

"Well... if you want to give it a try, go for it."

"I didn't know I needed your blessing." She laughed.

***

The next few weeks I was bogged down with exams, teaching, and social events. In mid-January, preparations began to welcome the

Chinese New Year—2002 was the Year of the Horse. The CCC organized a trip to the Harbin Ice Festival in northeast China. It was another one of those *wow* experiences. Hari was not on the trip, which surprised me. She never missed any travel offered by the group.

The IELTS exams kept me busy, as more and more Chinese were applying to go overseas. It had been an icy cold winter, and spring was a long time in coming. I hadn't seen Hari for over a month and guessed that she too was snowed under with work. I meant to call her but got distracted by other things.

While marking papers at the British Council one April afternoon, Hari came in and, tugging at my sleeve, said, "Let's have coffee. I'll treat you. I might even throw in a Danish."

"Hah! You know my secret—but you can't afford it. Especially the Danish," I joked.

"Oh, come on. Don't be such a sourpuss."

I followed her to the cafeteria with its gurgling coffee machine and its pervasive aroma. We sat down clasping our warm cups. Hari looked flushed and eager to talk. I knew her well enough to read her body language.

"Okay. Spit it out. What have you been up to?" I asked.

"Guilty as charged. I've gone and done it."

I was baffled. "Done what?"

"I joined Match.com."

"Good for you. When?"

"I did it soon after Toby left. For a while, I had no bites, but guess what! A couple of weeks ago I found someone, and we began corresponding."

"Wow! You're the secretive one. Why didn't you tell me?"

"I wasn't sure at first. I didn't want to be disappointed. Meeting someone in this virtual world can be tricky. It all seemed unreal to begin with."

"That's why you didn't come to the Harbin Ice Festival. Too busy being romanced by this guy," I said.

I was surprised but also happy for her. I peppered her with lots of questions—who was he? What did he look like? Where did he live? How old was he? Hari was only too eager to answer. His name was Edward and he was an engineer. He was from LA and currently working on an oil rig in the Middle East. This was his last contract, and then he would retire. Hari sounded happy.

"You should try internet dating. You never know who you might meet."

"I haven't got the time." I didn't want to dampen her enthusiasm by telling her that I wasn't comfortable trying to find romance online. Most of the expat men we encountered were either married or hooked up with younger Chinese women—there was a big pool of them, and readily available.

Another few weeks went by, and I was curious to know how her romance was progressing. We arranged to meet at one of the new restaurants near my apartment. Hari needed no prompting from me—she talked about Edward a lot during our lunch: his work, his emails, and his life overseas. It seemed he was quite smitten with her. I'd never seen her so chirpy.

As we were leaving, she said, "I had an email from a friend in England asking about some new virus outbreak here in China. We haven't been officially told, but you know how secretive they are. If it's true, the CCC will be cutting back on its travel program."

"Strange you should mention it," I said. "I too was asked the same thing by my cousin Nick in London. He's a retired doctor but keeps up with all things medical. I wonder if it's just a rumor or something we should know."

***

That was the beginning of rumors, denials, and the eventual admission by the government that this new "mystery" virus was called SARS—Severe Acute Respiratory Syndrome—a kind of atypical pneumonia that was deadly. The World Health Organization (WHO) broke the news that China and several of its neighboring countries were exporting it. Travelers to the Far East returned home sick. The mayor of Beijing went on air to assure us that there was no SARS in the capital and that the disease was confined to Guangdong province in the south. Beijing was safe, he said. In the meantime, WHO issued global alerts advising against travel to China and some of its neighboring countries.

My Chinese friend Esther called me late one evening and asked if she could visit. I was surprised but agreed. She came to my door dragging a heavy bag.

"Esther, what's the matter? You look all done in."

"I brought you food," she said, and with that, she opened the heavy sack that was full of rice. It must have contained at least fifty pounds. Food to the Chinese is rice. If there's no rice, there's no food.

"Esther, you didn't have to bring me rice."

"There's going to be a run on food. It's started already. Buy now before it's too late," she said.

Esther told me she was worried about her husband, who was a doctor.

"They called him to go to work four days ago. I haven't seen or heard from him since. I tried his cell phone, but he's not picking up."

She said that other doctors and medical staff had also been sequestered and were unable to contact their families. While the mayor was telling us that there was no SARS in Beijing, key workers were secretly taking out body bags under cover of darkness.

The government eventually admitted the existence and spread of SARS. A few weeks later, the mayor was sacked and blamed for mishandling the situation. Autocratic governments never admit to making mistakes; they find scapegoats instead. The mayor was the fall guy.

Esther was right. There was panic buying, and the shelves in the shops were empty. Beijing became a ghost city because the authorities "advised" citizens to stay home. Deciphering the official jargon and reading between the lines, it was obvious the government wanted us to stay put and not go out. The CCC ceased all activities, and IELTS exams were suspended. I hunkered down in my apartment, feeling bored and frustrated.

How long is this going to last?

I called Hari to see how she was doing. She told me she was in constant touch with Ed.

"So, it's Ed now? Short for Edward?"

"Yes. He calls me every day, sometimes twice. He's worried about me and wants to know if I'm safe. We talk for a long time, and I've gotten to know him really well. In some ways, SARS is a blessing as it gives me more free time to talk with him."

"So you're not keeping in touch online?" I asked.

"We do both. The internet is not always reliable. He's got my number and the reception is very good. It's as if he's in the next room. We've grown very close... We talk for hours. He must spend a fortune on these calls."

I could hear the excitement in her voice. Unlike me, she was not bored or frustrated with the lockdown. We hadn't actually been told not to leave our homes, but when the authorities "advise" and indicate they prefer you stay in your apartment, it's as good as an order. More or less.

At least Hari had Ed's phone calls to look forward to, and she kept pestering me.

"He's a great guy. Please let me ask him if he's got a twin or a friend for you too."

"I think I prefer to do my own fishing," I said.

Remembering Toby's words—*Nothing ventured, nothing gained*—I took the plunge. I signed up with Match.com and also with eHarmony. Why put all my eggs in one basket? The questionnaire I had to fill out for eHarmony was impressive—extremely detailed. It took me a couple of days to complete.

I'm not photogenic and I never like any pictures of myself. I found one photo of me astride a Bactrian camel in the Gobi Desert and posted it on both dating sites. Having ridden both Dromedary and Bactrian camels, I can vouch that the Bactrians are much easier to ride.

Nothing ventured, nothing gained.

Hari

***

After what seemed like a long time, travel restrictions were lifted and life resumed its usual rhythm. With an uptick in visa applications, we could hardly keep up with tests and exams. I wondered how Hari found time for hour-long chats with her beloved Ed.

Match.com was easier to navigate than eHarmony. I looked at some profiles but didn't feel I had an affinity with any of them. I had no time to waste browsing the internet, nor was I desperate to find that special someone. *My profile's out there—if anyone's interested, they can contact me.*

Meantime, Hari's relationship with Ed was in full bloom—they were already planning a future together. Every time his name came up, her face lit up. She was in love.

One morning over coffee, Hari broke the news that she was going to New York to help her daughter, who was going through a divorce.

"Her husband's left her, and she's trying to cope. She's got a full-time job and she's struggling to be a single mom with three kids under ten. She's having a rough time."

"I'm sorry to hear that. How awful! What happened?"

"They had problems in the past, but they seemed happy the last few years. Then he found someone else, and he wants out of the marriage. I need to be there for her. She asked me to come... Ed is planning to come to New York too. He's nearing the end of his contract, and I want him to meet my family."

I told Hari I'd be leaving for London soon myself.

"I find Beijing too hot and uncomfortable in the summer. I'm ready to pay off my mortgage, and I need to find new tenants for my house."

"Good for you!" Hari said. "And remember to let me know about your internet dating. I so wish you'll find someone like my Ed. He asked me to marry him soon after we met online. That's why I look forward to our first meeting in New York."

"Okay. I'll keep you updated. And don't forget to invite me to the wedding."

"I definitely will," she promised. "You'll be my matron of honor. We shared so much over the past three years—so many adventures. Remember when we said we'd collect memories here in China? Well, we certainly have!"

I nodded in agreement. I knew it would be some time before we met again.

***

My home in London had been trashed by a tenant who stopped paying rent and had become a squatter. The management company that was supposed to take care of things had let me down. It took a while to repair the damage, but at the same time, I had the great satisfaction of paying off the mortgage. The house was now mine, and

I had the deeds to prove it. All those hours of hard work in China had paid off. In between fixing up my home and catching up with friends, I indulged my love for classical music and opera with my cousin Nick, who shared my interests.

"When I heard of SARS, I was really worried about you," Nick said.

"Actually, it wasn't as bad as we thought at the time. Of course, people died, and the government tried to brush it under the carpet, but it didn't last long."

"Nevertheless, I'm glad you're home now."

"It's strange hearing the word *home* because I really miss China. Once the repairs are done, I might go back," I said.

"Why do you want to go back? You accomplished what you set out to do. You're now debt-free and solvent. Why go back?"

He wasn't keen for me to leave. I had a sneaky suspicion that he didn't want to lose his concert buddy. He had never married and didn't know how to cook. Whenever he came to my house, he'd ask me to make him an omelet—filled with veggies, cheese, and anything else I happened to have handy. He was good company and always kind to me.

The house repairs were costly and took longer than I expected. Ruth, a neighbor, called one morning and asked me if I was interested in teaching English to immigrants.

"The local council is looking for teachers for adult immigrants, who are here legally and waiting to get their citizenship. They need to have sufficient English for their interviews. They've been advertising for several weeks now."

"Sounds like the work I did in China. I'll check it out," I said and thanked her. I was still undecided whether I was going to stay or return to Beijing. Since I had nothing to lose, I contacted the local council. Within a week, I had a job.

Hari kept in touch by email. Though busy helping her daughter in New York, she looked forward to Ed's arrival. He was wrapping up his last contract in the Emirates and planned to fly to the Big Apple to meet her.

"I look forward to a new life and a new beginning with him," she wrote.

She asked how my internet dating was going. She often ended her emails with: "I so wish you'd meet someone like my Ed. He's truly amazing. You too deserve to be happy."

***

Toby also wanted to know if I had found someone special online. I never asked what happened to the two guys she dated online while she visited me in China. After all those dives into Beijing's Internet cafés, she had found her man through a blind date. Since both Hari and Toby wanted to know about my dating progress, I shared some of my online adventures.

I did get some hits eventually, but nothing came of them. However, I learned something from each encounter. The first lesson was to never ignore red flags—such as with the guy who wrote, *"You'd better not argue with me,"* and who booked the honeymoon suite at the Raffles Hotel in Singapore as a "surprise."

The second lesson I learned was to eliminate people who send only pretty e-cards and inspirational forwards written by others. When I asked one to describe his town, he could hardly spell or write a coherent sentence.

The third lesson was to read between the lines—to look for what was left unsaid or vague. I learned this from Don, who told me he was cured of Guillain-Barré Syndrome. Doing my own research, I found out that this is an incurable and progressive disease—cousin Nick said as much. Don was looking for a nurse/girlfriend. When I told him that I could not fulfill that role, he became angry—that too was another red flag.

I approached all contacts with a cocktail of respect, nonchalance, and a good dose of skepticism—well shaken and stirred. I made short shrift of those who failed to meet my criteria. After three or four encounters, I learned to separate the wheat from the chaff. So far, it was mostly chaff—twerps, jerks, scammers, lechers, and leeches. I let them down gently, explaining that *"I wasn't good enough for them,"* or *"I could not meet their high standards."* It was safer and easier to bow out gracefully.

Men have fragile egos—some more than others. I kept the real reasons for turning them down—my rejection slips—to myself. After a few months, I acquired a rich collection. Here's a small sample of them:

Seriously, you expect me to move to Montana and take care of you and your 96-year-old mother?

I'm honored that you consider me a helpmeet and that you'll thrive on my baking. It ain't gonna happen.

Are you kidding me, when you say that my place is in the home and as a dutiful wife I have to submit to your authority?

I'm flattered you find me sexy and desirable—if you shaved all that hair off your face I might be able to reciprocate your feelings.

No, I don't talk dirty and I'm not interested in relieving your sexual frustrations.

You want me to pay for your airfare to come meet me in London?

What do you mean it's a loan? Since when do I have to loan you money for "our" dream home/holiday/yacht? Dream on, jerk!

I'm sorry you're in a bind, but I can't send you three thousand dollars as a temporary loan.

Some were nice, decent men, but not my cup of tea. Like the man who kept asking about King Arthur and the Knights of the Round Table.

He was obsessed with that legend, so I told him I had never met any of the knights, but that I'd seen the Seven Dwarfs in the New Forest.

Then there was the guy who wanted to know about Stonehenge and kept on and on about it, until I told him that during the winter solstice, my coven and I danced naked there in the moonlight. If they couldn't take a joke, that was a no-no.

While still undecided as to whether to return to China or remain in London, eHarmony came up with a match. His name was Charles, from Payson, Arizona. From his profile picture, he looked like a hippie from the sixties—with long hair and a longer beard. I shot him one line:

"Hi, I live in London. I worked for the BBC and I'm now teaching English to immigrants."

He was a retired school superintendent. *If he's in education, then he can spell.* I wouldn't have to correct his English. I had already met too many "suitors," mostly from the US, who maintained they had master's degrees but could hardly spell or express themselves on paper.

Charles replied right away. He was a widower with one son. The son was married and lived in another state. Over several weeks and many emails, we discovered that we had a great deal in common—books, politics, religion, and travel.

Hari

Before I knew it, Charles—who went by Chuck (Americans love to abbreviate or change their names)—was coming to London to meet me.

He's in a hurry. We just started corresponding. How do I introduce him to my family and friends?

I had already told Toby and Hari about Chuck, but not Nick, who was my closest relative. I knew he would not share their enthusiasm, as he considered all things American inferior. To him, London was the center of the universe, and choosing to live anywhere else was unthinkable.

***

I met Chuck at Heathrow Airport one bright sunny morning on 30th April 2007. I acted as his guide around London. We went to the National Gallery and the British Museum, took in a show in the West End, and had high tea at my club. He was a true gentleman with impeccable manners. I noticed how he always walked on the roadside of the sidewalk, opened doors for me, was clean and tidy, and soft-spoken. And he *listened.* He said he loved to listen to me talk—I know I'm loquacious—I love to talk. Talkers love listeners, and Chuck was a good listener.

Five days after he arrived, he got down on one knee and proposed.

"But… you don't know me," I said.

"I know enough."

For some reason, I said *yes.*

Easter was upon us. Most years, Nick and a few close family and friends came to my place for the traditional lamb and desserts. But aside from culinary delights, this time I had to present Chuck to them. How was I to introduce him? I was in a quandary. I discussed my dilemma with him.

"Why not tell them the truth? That we're engaged. I've already told my family."

"But we haven't made definite plans—where we're going to live, when and where the wedding will take place. They'll want to know."

"We'll take all their questions as they come."

His response calmed me. I was indeed happy to have him in my life. Now I could concentrate on preparing for Easter—and also for my trip to Payson with Chuck.

My going to Payson was Chuck's idea.

"Why not come and see where I live? You've never been to the States, and I think it's a good idea if you see beforehand what you're letting yourself in for," he said.

"Aren't you worried I might change my mind?"

"It's a risk I'll have to take," he chuckled.

Easter preparations, followed by Easter Sunday, went by quickly. We announced our engagement to my guests. Cousin Nick did not make a scene. He simply muttered, "If you're happy, I'm happy for you too."

I managed to book my trip to the United States on the same flight as Chuck. Serendipity worked her magic again.

***

We flew to Phoenix and then drove the ninety miles to Payson. I had an open return ticket, as I planned to stop in New York on my way back to visit Hari. I had taken two weeks 'leave of absence from my job. Chuck hoped that I'd stay longer. He was disappointed I couldn't extend my visit.

"There's so much I want to show you," he said.

"I know. But I can't take more leave. I still have to see to those final repairs to my house."

Chuck's place was a craftsman-style house, a little outside the town center. It was spacious, with a big deck on three sides and surrounded by trees—bucolic and very quiet. He and his late wife had it built as their retirement home, but she didn't live long enough to enjoy it.

Chuck was a wonderful host. We drove to Flagstaff and from there took the train to the Grand Canyon. We visited the Petrified Forest National Park and then Central City in Colorado. That was a long trip. I hadn't realized how big the country was. Chuck was right—there was a lot to see, and not enough time.

Two days before my return flight, Chuck invited some of his friends and neighbors for a barbecue. Everyone arrived with a dish. That was my introduction to the wonderful potluck tradition. It seemed as if half of Payson was there. I wondered whether they came to see the English fiancée Chuck had found on the internet. We still hadn't decided where we'd live, or how we would combine and manage our finances and households. We hadn't even set a time or place for our wedding.

The evening before my flight, Chuck looked sad. "You're very quiet," he said. "What's on your mind?"

"I had a wonderful time, and I'm glad I came. It's all been very interesting. You've introduced me to a country and a world I did not know."

"So how do you feel about moving to the US? Do you think you can make that leap across the pond and live here with me?"

I had expected that question. During my visit, he was keen to show me the best his country had to offer. He was a great guy—good, kind, and uncomplicated—but I felt unable to give him a definite *yes* at that moment.

"You know, there are so many things we need to sort out. Stuff I have to deal with before I make that leap. Have you thought about coming to live in London?"

He looked crestfallen. "I did think about it, but financially it'd be impossible. I can't afford to live in London."

"Well... let's not make any hasty decisions. Let's put our thinking caps on. We need more time before we finalize our plans."

"I don't want to lose you," he sighed. "You're not saying farewell, are you?" And he reached for my hand.

The next day, he drove me to the airport where we parted in sweet sorrow. I had a two-day stop in New York to meet up with Hari before returning to London. On the plane, I settled into my seat, buckled up, and tried to relax. I was looking forward to seeing Hari again, but my mind was working overtime. There were too many life-changing decisions and no easy answers. Finally, I dozed off until we landed at JFK Airport.

Hari had recommended a hotel close to her daughter's house. After I checked in, I called her. She arrived in no time. It was as if we had never been apart. She looked great. She had lost some weight but still had the same sparkle in her eyes and girlish giggle.

"You're having brunch with us tomorrow. My daughter's looking forward to meeting you," she said, "but it can be a bit noisy with the kids around. I thought it best to have some time on our own."

We had a lot of catching up to do. I wanted to hear about Ed, and she wanted to know about Chuck. I asked her when Ed would be coming, and she said it couldn't be soon enough.

"He's truly amazing. He knows about my daughter and her situation. And he said that he'd take care of all of us."

"Wow! That's very generous of him. I can understand why you love him so much."

"That's the reason he's working so hard on this last contract. It will enable him to retire with a tidy sum so that I and the 'girls, 'as he calls us, will have nothing to worry about. Now tell me about your guy. How was your visit to Arizona?"

"Everyone was very kind. We visited some interesting places, and I got to see and meet Chuck's home and his friends."

Hari raised an eyebrow. "Somehow I can hear a big *but* in there," she said. She could read me like a book. "I sense you have second thoughts, and I think I can understand some of them. You're a city girl. I wondered how you'd settle in a rural environment, in a small town like Payson."

"I tried to see myself living there. It's so different from my life in London and Beijing. When I met his friends, I realized I had nothing in common with them. They're nice people, but all they can talk about is their kids or grandkids. One or two asked how dangerous it must have been living in a communist country like China—but they weren't really interested."

"Yup. Anything they don't understand here in the US they label *socialism.* It's their bogeyman. It's actually ignorance."

"I asked Chuck if he'd consider living in London. He said he couldn't afford it."

Hari said, "He's fifteen years your senior. That generation raised their men to be providers and the women to be homemakers—a very clear gender divide in roles. He feels he'd be failing his God-ordained role if he couldn't support you."

"I sensed that. Coming here and seeing him in his own environment was an eye-opener. I'll have to give it some serious thought."

"Don't rush into anything. Give yourself time to think. Come visit again if necessary."

We talked late into the night. The following day, I visited her home, where I met her attorney daughter, Emily, and her three grandchildren. I was glad that Ed would join this little family and take good care of them. She had found her knight in shining armor.

Later that evening, she saw me off at the airport and reminded me of my promise to be her matron of honor.

"It'd be an honor," I said.

***

London felt more like home now. I enjoyed fixing up my house, and my new job enabled me to make more upgrades than I'd originally planned. Chuck and I kept in touch daily via email and phone. To his credit, he didn't press me for an answer, for which I was grateful.

A month after I returned, I was asked if I was interested in applying for a vacancy coming up with my local district council as head of the department dealing with immigrant affairs. I'd be doubling my salary—and my responsibilities. After some hesitation, I applied and was successful. I got the job. Then I told Chuck.

Of course, he wasn't happy. He felt I was putting down roots in London at a time when I should be thinking about packing up and leaving for the States. Cousin Nick was pleased, though.

"If you go there, you'll be bored out of your mind," he said. "What are you going to do in a small rural town, where its only claim to fame is a rodeo? I can't see you going to hoedowns and dancing to hillbilly music. It'd grate on your classical music-loving ears. Once the novelty wears off, you'll miss everything you enjoy here in London— the opera, concerts, galleries. Your very soul will starve."

He was unaware of the fact that he was echoing some of my own thoughts. I loved Chuck and I didn't want to hurt him. The more I thought about it, the more confused I became. I was filled with doubts and hesitation. As if sensing my dilemma, Chuck called and assured me of his love.

"I know this is a major change for you," he said. "No pressure from me… take your time. I miss you terribly, and I want us to be together, but you have to be happy with your decision. Your happiness is important to me."

His kindness and understanding made it even harder to decide. Like a pendulum, my life was swinging back and forth—stay or go, London or Payson, rural living or cosmopolitan city life? At least Chuck had allowed me a short reprieve. I immersed myself in my new job and put my decision regarding our future together on hold.

***

September that year came with an Indian summer. I was tired of Nick's constant criticism and put-downs of all things American— people, culture, and politics. If he was trying to convince me that going to the States was a mistake, he was doing it the wrong way.

"Why are you so judgmental?" I shouted at him one day. "Don't be such a snob! Just because people don't enjoy the same things you do, or have different lifestyles and worldviews, doesn't mean they're inferior. They have a right to their ways, just as you have to yours. One of the many things I enjoy when I travel is that I learn about different cultures. Variety is the spice of life. If I married someone like myself, I'd be bored to death."

I didn't need Nick's negative input in my life. I had some leave coming. On impulse, I booked a flight to New York and emailed Hari.

"I can't wait," she replied. "This time I'll show you around New York."

***

I booked the same hotel as before and called Hari. As soon as we met, Hari wanted to know about Chuck. I confessed I hadn't told him I was visiting New York.

"You were right," I said. "Best to think things through. This new job is taking up a lot of my time and energy. I've spent a great deal of money fixing up my house, I'm loath to leave it or rent it out again."

Then I asked her about Ed. "You've been dating and planning a life with him for almost a year now," I said. "Why is it taking so long? What's the holdup?"

"He's had some problems at work, and things have not worked out as he expected, causing delays."

"Do you have any idea when he might be coming?"

"Soon, I hope. I just wired him $40,000 to finish the job in Dubai and leave," she said.

"You did *what*?" I was incredulous. "Why?"

She was quick to reassure me. "It's only a loan. His bank has blocked his money, so he can't access it. I'm helping him until it gets sorted."

"I don't understand. I thought he was well paid for working on an oil rig. You told me he was saving for retirement and coming to take care of you and your family."

My head was spinning. I wanted to make sure I understood what she was telling me, but somehow I couldn't connect the dots.

"I saw his bank account," Hari said. "He's got a great deal of money there. He just can't access it. That's why I'm helping him—to speed things up."

"How long has this been going on?"

"It started several months ago. He asked me to help. He even gave me access to his account. He was very upfront and honest."

All the red flags I'd collected during my internet dating encounters popped up. Hari was convinced that she was doing the right thing, and I didn't want to scare her. At the same time, I wanted to help her. *Gently does it.* She's vulnerable. She's so besotted with him. $40,000 is a lot of money. *What for?*

"Let's go get a drink at the bar. We'll find a quiet corner and you can tell me all about it." I kept a straight face and my voice calm. *What has she got herself into?* Right now, I could certainly do with a drink myself.

We found a quiet nook and settled down with our drinks. I began asking what the problem was, and Hari was only too happy to fill me in. It seems that soon after they met online and started "dating," Ed said he needed to purchase some equipment for his job. When he tried to access his account in LA, it was blocked. Time was running out. He needed the funds urgently, or he'd lose the contract. He asked Hari to help him.

"So this recent payment of $40,000 was not the first time you sent him money?" I asked.

"Oh no! I've loaned him quite a lot—actually, most of my savings."

"What? How much?"

"Around $300,000. But it's only a loan. He's got a couple of million dollars in his blocked account. I *saw* it. It's so typical of banks—they urge you to deposit money with them, and the minute you need to withdraw it, they make it difficult. It's just a temporary thing. Once Ed gets here, he'll sort it out."

I was flabbergasted. He "allowed" her to look into his finances, where he had apparently stashed his millions, then pleaded for an advance to help him out. She called it a "loan." But this is *three hundred thousand dollars* we're talking about. Some loan! I couldn't hold back my suspicions anymore.

"Hari, are you sure this isn't a scam?"

"Oh no! How can you think that? I talked with Ed's son. He has a nice family in Texas. And I also talked with a friend of Ed's from his schooldays."

"What kind of people are they? What did they look like when you spoke with them?" I asked.

"I never got to see them. It was done online. Just like with Ed."

Hari

"You mean you never see Ed visually when you speak to him online? You have no video?"

"He sent me his picture, but since he's on an oil rig somewhere in the Persian Gulf, reception is not always good. We have no visual, but I know what he looks like from his photograph."

I began to think more and more that my friend had fallen prey to romance scammers. How could she be so naive? The contact with the so-called "family" in Texas was also without visual. Their excuse was that their computer camera didn't work. I was dumbfounded.

"My daughter, Emily, is now dating a nice guy from her office. They're getting serious, and he might move in with her. If that happens, I'll be in their way. I sent this last payment to Ed to speed up the conclusion of his contract."

"Did you get him to sign a contract for the money you loaned him?" I already knew the answer before she replied.

"No. I know he's not short of funds. It's just a temporary glitch until he gets here."

I was still trying to understand how she could be so reckless. This was not the Hari I knew. What happened to the shrewd, savvy, and frugal Hari of our Beijing days?

"You said he sent you his picture?"

"Yes, several—including his passport with his picture in it. We're planning to move to LA, where he has a house. I don't have to stay in

145

New York for my daughter now. I'm really looking forward to a new life with him. He makes me feel safe and loved. I haven't felt like this for a long time. Not since my husband died."

She was now thinking with her emotions, not her head. Love had blinded her and made her reckless. But to the tune of *three hundred thousand dollars?* Something's wrong.

"I hate to say this, but I'm not comfortable with Ed's need for you to bail him out of his money problems. Why hasn't he gone to his son, or somebody else for help?"

"He did, but they couldn't raise that much capital in a hurry. It was important that Ed got the money quickly or he'd lose the contract."

"I can't understand how someone who has millions in his account has it blocked. And why would he have so much money in a regular bank account? Do you know the reason?"

Hari wasn't clear—or didn't even fully understand—the reason for Ed's urgent need for money, or why the bank had blocked his account. The more I prodded, the more vague her answers became. It was obvious she had bought his story hook, line, and sinker. As we continued to talk, I sensed fear overcoming her. *Does she realize she's been had?* She looked worried. *Perhaps the penny's dropped.*

"Does your daughter know how much money you've given this man?"

"No, she doesn't. I even borrowed some from her, because this last payment cleaned me out."

Suddenly she changed the topic.

"Anyway, tomorrow I'm going to be your guide around New York. First stop is Astoria, in Queens."

She looked uncomfortable. I thought it best to drop the subject. But before we parted for the night, I made her promise that she'd text me Ed's passport picture, his son's phone number, and his home address in LA.

I was determined to do my own sleuthing.

***

The next couple of days were packed with sightseeing tours and visits to interesting places. Hari had planned a rich program, which included Ellis Island, Queens, a walking tour of Greenwich Village, and a quick visit to the Guggenheim. If Hari was trying to wear me out, she succeeded. I also noticed a change in her—she was quiet. Usually, her bubbly personality enveloped everything around her. I wondered whether she was mulling over my warning about being scammed. She hardly mentioned Ed during our tours, which was so unlike her.

On the third day, I pleaded with Hari to take a rain check. "I'm exhausted. My feet are killing me. I need to rest."

"No problem. Emily asked if you'd like to come over for dinner tomorrow, say around six, and meet her new friend. His name's Rick. I think you'll like him."

"Okay. I'll see you tomorrow."

Hari had already texted me the information I'd asked regarding Ed. I now had his passport photo, his son's telephone number, and his home address in Los Angeles. Remembering that Pacific Time is three hours behind Eastern Time, I decided to wait until noon before I called my friend Toby in LA. There was no need. She called me.

"Hey, Nora. I did check out the address you sent."

"Oh yes? What time is it in your neck of the woods?"

"It's seven in the morning, but I didn't want to wait any longer. Here's what I found out: the address you gave me is wrong. There's no house with that number on that street. Are you sure you have the right address?"

"Yes. This is the address that Ed gave to Hari. He said it's where his house is."

"That's not a residential area. It's a long road with a lot of empty lots. It's wrong."

I was on the horns of a dilemma. I didn't know how much of my suspicions I should share with Toby. When she and Hari first met at my home in Beijing, they got on like a house on fire—but this was

Hari's story and Hari's business. On the other hand, I needed Toby's help.

"Toby, I think Hari is the victim of a romance scammer."

"You mean Ed? She told me about him and looks forward to coming here to be with him in LA. I told her she could stay with me if she wanted."

I sighed with relief. At least Toby knew part of the story. As I recounted my suspicions, I could hear Toby go "OMG" at frequent intervals. I didn't specify how much money Hari had sent to this "Ed." It wasn't necessary. Toby got the picture. It was as if a huge burden had been lifted from me by sharing what I suspected.

"Did you say you have a picture of this guy?"

"Yes. A couple, including his passport photo," I said.

"Okay. That's good. My niece works at the passport fraud office in Washington. She joined the State Department right after college and hasn't looked back since. She's a bright kid. Send me his passport page with his picture and I'll get her to investigate."

"I'm sending it as we speak. In the meantime, I'll call the son's number in Texas. Thanks, Toby. I hope we'll get to the bottom of this. By the way, Hari doesn't know I'm doing this."

"I feel so sorry for her. It's so not like her."

I hung up and called the number Hari had given me for the son. All I got was, *"This number is no longer available."* Another piece of evidence in this ugly puzzle. I had a sick feeling in the pit of my stomach. I'd better pull myself together before dinner tonight with Hari's family. I can't mention the scam, the lost money, or Ed in front of Emily and Rick. Let Hari play happy families with them a while longer. I need strength.

I went down to the hotel restaurant and ordered a salad. The waiter brought me a glass of red wine.

"Waiter, I didn't order this."

"It's from the gentleman sitting at the bar, ma'am. With his compliments."

I took the glass and smelled its bouquet. Hmm. Not a very good or expensive one. Rather mediocre. I asked the waiter to box my salad. I drank most of the wine, then turned and raised the glass to the man in the blue sweater at the bar. I left the dining room without a second glance. *There's one lurking behind every corner, on every bar stool and every social platform. If you think you can impress me with a glass of cheap wine, you've got another thing coming.*

The food tasted better in my room. Then I took a much-needed nap.

Buzzing from my phone woke me up. It was Hari, wondering if I'd forgotten our dinner date. I rushed to get ready and got a taxi to her place, half an hour late. I instantly liked Rick, Emily's friend, and realized that if he moved in, her mother would feel in the way. I was racking my mind for an excuse to have a private chat with Hari when she said:

"I'm so sorry. I forgot. I have a dental appointment tomorrow morning. Can we meet in the afternoon? Is there somewhere special you'd like to go or see?"

That was my cue.

"How about a Chinese meal before I leave—to remind us of our time in Beijing?"

"Great idea. I know just the place. I'll be done by noon. How about meeting in your hotel lobby at two? It's not very far, about ten minutes 'drive."

"Can you make it a little later?" I had my reasons for the delay. "Let's make it an early dinner. How about five?"

"Sure. Five o'clock it is then."

***

I needed the extra few hours to get more information. I wanted to gather all the facts and data I could on this type of fraud. I also hoped that Toby's niece might come back to us soon regarding the passport photograph. Adrenaline pulsed through my body, providing a mixture of excitement and fear. Half my brain was thinking, *Don't get involved,* and the other half was saying, *Get as much information as you can to help your friend. She's been taken to the cleaners.* The ambivalence added to the high I felt. I was doing a fine balancing act. I also felt guilty about Chuck, who thought I was still in London. At least Chuck was real. I had met him, been to his house, and he'd never asked me for money—whereas Hari's Ed remained unseen and out of reach.

By six o'clock the next morning, I was in the hotel's computer room. I needed to use one of their large-screen computers and printer, as well as my laptop. Luckily, no one else was there. For several hours, I researched, looked up, and gathered useful data. There was a ton of information out there on the web—all I had to do was tap into it—link after link after link. I hadn't realized how prevalent this type of scam was until now. Google, Twitter, Facebook, and YouTube were my partners, associates, and helpers. They churned out an enormous amount of evidence proving that romance scamming is on the rise and highly profitable for the perpetrators. It's a multi-million-dollar business targeting vulnerable people. They phish for their prey on social media, dating sites, small ads, and business connections. Their targets tend to be older, lonely men and women looking for love.

Victims become enmeshed in a cocoon, spun carefully with lies and false promises, and are held captive while their bank accounts are being depleted. Hari was not alone. Hundreds like her fall for these predators. The fraudsters use well-rehearsed scripts and sometimes work in groups. Many are based in West Africa, Russia, or Asia.

In Hari's case, she'd been introduced to a "son" and his "family," and also to another "friend" who called her to tell her what a great person

Ed was, and how wonderful she was to help him. She'd been sold a fantasy, swept off her feet by a man promising love and companionship. He had discovered all her weak spots and emotional needs. She believed Ed's lie that a new, happy life lay ahead for them.

The MO was familiar: hit on a needy, lonely woman, declare undying love and devotion, make up a reason for your lack of visual contact—poor weather conditions on an oil rig, working undercover on a top-secret mission—followed by one hard-luck disaster after another. Men also fall prey to these scams. The common denominator is the urgent need for money because their funds are temporarily unavailable. They produce fake bank accounts showing balances of thousands or millions of dollars, but due to a glitch, they cannot access them. Another common feature of this type of fraud is that they never, or hardly ever, meet face-to-face with their victims. Some "disaster" befalls the scammer, causing delays and the need for more money. Some scams drag on for months, even years.

The previous night, I'd asked the concierge to get me an extra ream of paper, knowing I'd need a lot. I printed out all the information I had unearthed. Toby's call came at two o'clock. Her niece's findings did not surprise me. She said the passport was fake, and so was the picture. She'd done a Google reverse image search and discovered that "Ed's" photograph was, in fact, that of a retired U.S. Army colonel. His name was Oliver Bruce Hoffman—married—and he lived in North Carolina. I printed that information, too, along with Hoffman's picture.

Collecting all the data was one thing. Now I faced the most difficult part: how to break the news to Hari and burst the bubble of delusion she had lived in for so long. I would be destroying her hopes, dreams, and love for a man who didn't even exist. I called Toby back to explain my dilemma. She was supportive, insisting that Hari should be told the truth. Ultimately, it would be up to her—whether to believe it, and what to do. The facts spoke for themselves, but she still remained to be convinced.

I was putting our friendship on the line.

***

I met Hari in the hotel lobby. I had been hunched over those computers for hours; my back ached, my eyes were sore, and I felt ill at ease. Instead of my usual small purse, I strapped a leather briefcase over my shoulder and tried to make it look like a normal fashion accessory. It contained the printouts and all the info I had gathered earlier in the day. Hari had chosen a great restaurant that brought back memories of our time in Beijing. She asked after Chuck, and I told her that I hadn't heard from him for a couple of days, which was surprising. I sensed this was the opening I needed. "Have you heard from Ed again?"

"Actually, yes, I have. I had an email last night, and he tried to call me this morning as I was leaving for the dentist. Something strange happened."

"What was it?" I asked.

"He'd finished his job and was getting off the rig. He'd packed all his stuff in his big suitcase, and as it was being lifted off the platform, the winch broke, and all his belongings fell into the sea. He lost everything—clothes, passport, wallet, ID documents, even his air tickets to New York."

I didn't know whether to laugh or simply ask: How much does he want this time? I managed to control myself. I said, "So, what's going to happen now?"

Just then, our Peking duck arrived; Hari busied herself passing me the pancakes and all the bits and pieces that go with this classic dish. I sat there watching her and waited, while my mind was screaming: How much? How much?

She looked thoughtful and sad. "He said he needed money to pay for a hotel room, and a new airfare, while the embassy worked on getting him a new passport, and that it'd take time. He said being without ID was dangerous in those countries." Why am I not surprised? This is almost identical to some of the scenarios I read about this morning.

"How much does he need?" I was careful to use the word "need" and not "want."

"He said thirty thousand dollars until he can get money from his own bank account."

"Have you sent him the money?"

"No. Not yet. I didn't have time to go to my bank. Besides, I don't think I have that much left."

"Okay. Let's enjoy our meal, then head back to my hotel for a nightcap, and we'll talk about it." I was giving myself time to think. Best to expose this fraudster in a less public and noisy environment––a quiet hotel lounge or my room.

On the way back to my hotel, Hari said, "I don't think I can ask my daughter for an advance," and looked at me.

I hope she's not going to ask me for a loan.

The hotel lounge was almost empty. I chose a corner booth with a large table. This could not wait any longer. The moment for truth had come. "Hari, I have some information to share with you. I don't know how you'll take it, but I want you to listen carefully and see what I have to show you here."

"Do you remember when I asked you if you'd been scammed? You told me that you had talked with Ed's son and another friend of his and that he'd sent you his address in LA?"

She nodded. I told her that Toby had checked the address Ed had given her and that it was fake—there was no such number or house on that street. I also told her that the son's telephone number was no longer available. If she doubted me, all she had to do was call it. She remained silent.

"Hari, you do believe me, don't you? To give this man so much money, and not even be able to see him while you speak online or on the phone, is very suspicious."

"It's not easy with poor weather conditions in the Persian Gulf. Even our voice communications get interrupted," she said, trying to defend the indefensible.

It was obvious that my news was not welcome and she didn't want to believe that she'd been scammed. I was careful to avoid using words like naive, foolish, stupid, and desperate, to describe her actions. I knew the time would come when she'd own them and beat herself with them. I left the most important revelation for last. "Hari, I had Ed's photograph and passport checked by the passport fraud office in D.C. They are fake." She gasped.

"The picture you have is not Ed's photo. It belongs to a retired army colonel. His name is Oliver Bruce Hoffman, and he lives in North Carolina with his wife."

"No! What are you talking about? It can't be true!" The shock was now visible all over her face. I handed her the information from Toby's niece. She shook her head in disbelief.

"Hari, I know this is a lot to take in. I want you to take all this information home with you. Check out the son's and friend's contact numbers. Go to your bank and change all your passwords. Here's a checklist I want you to look at. I've listed the ways these scammers operate. Tick the boxes that pertain to your relationship with this Ed.

These crooks use the same MO. They even lift words and sentences from social media. They use words like 'babe 'or 'I need your help, ' and you can find many of them on Facebook."

A look of disbelief came over her. I wondered whether it was disbelief at my information or realization that she'd been conned in the most cruel way.

I was about to return to London and did not want to leave her in limbo. I had prepared a long checklist with boxes for her to tick off and copied all the relevant links so that she could fact-check them herself. I knew that if she challenged him at this stage, he'd tell her I was lying or that my information was wrong. And he'd reassure her—again and again—of his undying love and utter devotion. I could almost play the scenario in my mind:

"Oh, babe. After all this time, how can you not trust me? You're my sun, my everything. I can't live without you. You're my one and only. Don't listen to lies and false accusations. I'd never do anything to hurt you."

And she'd believe him—because, deep down, she *wants* to believe him.

"Hari, promise me you'll look over the data and the links I had put together. They deal with identical cases—just like yours. I've even referred you to sites from which these scammers lift whole sentences, and how they phish on the internet. They cast their nets wide— hundreds of castings at a time—and once they catch their prey, they reel them in. The checklist should help you. Read and check everything, and then you decide how you want to proceed."

At this point, Hari's face was ashen, and her hands were shaking.

"Yes, I did notice an accent, and his spelling wasn't great. He said he was dyslexic," she whispered.

So he'd covered all the bases.

"How soon after you first met online did he express his undying love for you?"

"I can't remember, but it was soon after we got off Match.com and started using our personal emails."

"Okay. That's another *yes* on the checklist," I said as gently as possible.

"Believe me, I'm not enjoying this—and I was in two minds about whether to tell you or not. I know I'm putting our friendship on the line here, but I'd be a poor friend if I didn't tell you the truth."

Her pain made me angry. This con man had promised her the earth. He'd won her trust and love with lies. I wished there was a way I could spare her this. I asked her to share her story with her daughter, not keep it hidden, and to stop all communication with him. I couldn't hold out any hope of her getting back the money, but I strongly advised her to report him to the FBI.

She was stunned and hardly said a word, but her eyes and demeanor spoke volumes. I offered to ride back in the taxi with her, but she declined. She walked out into the night like a somnambulist.

I slept fitfully, with Hari's tearful face haunting my dreams. I had some last-minute shopping to do before leaving later that evening. Hari called as I was about to go for breakfast.

"I don't want you to leave without seeing you," she said. "I know you mean well, but I can't get my head around this. All those lies... All those promises. I just can't believe it."

"It'll take a while for the whole thing to sink in. Remember how you told me to take things slow and easy with Chuck? In your case it's just the opposite—it should be fast and final. You have all the evidence Toby and I gathered, plus the emails and phone calls, as well as bank statements. Please go to the FBI and report this fraudster." I could almost hear the silence at the other end of the line. "Why don't we meet here for a late lunch? I have some errands to do this morning, but I'll be back around two-thirty to finish packing. How about three o'clock at the restaurant downstairs?"

She agreed. It would be a bittersweet meeting, but I was glad I was going to see her before leaving for London.

***

Much as I enjoy overseas travel, it's always good to return home. I had told Hari she could come stay with me whenever she wished. Toby had said the same about LA.

A few days after I got back, Toby emailed to say Hari was visiting her in LA. She insisted on being shown the street where "Ed" said he lived. Toby drove her there.

"I guess she wanted proof positive," Toby said, "that the house she had dreamed of and hoped to share with 'Ed, 'didn't exist. I also showed her, again, the email my niece sent about the passport and its photo. I had a hard time convincing her that she'd been conned, but at least she's not sending him money anymore. It's so sad to see her like this. She feels ashamed and embarrassed. Anyway, how are you and Chuck coming along? Have you decided about relocating to the States?"

I hadn't heard from Chuck for over a week, which was strange. I'd been so engrossed in Hari's problems I had neglected him. I called a couple of times, but there was only a voicemail asking me to leave a message, and my emails remained unanswered. I wondered whether he'd heard I'd been to New York and was offended.

I wanted to invite him to spend Christmas with me in London. I've always loved that time of year. There is so much to do and enjoy. London becomes a fairy wonderland with spectacular decorations and overhead lights strewn along Oxford and Regent Streets. Every department store, from Harrods to Selfridges, vies to create the best-dressed window displays. West End theaters put on their best productions, from musicals to dramas, comedies, and pantomimes.

I wanted to share it all with Chuck. Besides, I missed him. He made me feel happy and safe when we were together.

Am I suffering from the fallout from Hari's disaster? Maybe. I too feel lonely and need to have someone to share my life with. Those thoughts made me long even more to have Chuck share the holidays with me. I'll ask him to come and spend the Christmas season here in London. Perhaps he can even stay until the Chinese New Year. I began looking up places we could visit together. Oxford would be on the list, as well as some of the beautiful hamlets and towns along the Thames.

The thought of his coming cheered me up. All I had to do now was call him and invite him over.

I already felt uplifted and energized by my decision.

***

It was a bright, sunny Sunday morning when Chuck's son, Jonathan, called to tell me that Chuck had passed away, having lost his battle with cancer. I was stunned.

"What? When did this happen? I had no idea."

"I found your messages on his answering machine, and gathered you hadn't heard," he said gently.

"What? When did this happen? I didn't know he had cancer. It can't be. I don't understand."

"Dad asked me to tell you that he's mailed you a letter explaining everything. He also asked me to let you have his early edition Mark Twain books, which I'll do."

My head was spinning. Was I hearing right? He continued speaking and I wanted to turn off the sound of his voice.

"I'm so sorry you didn't have more time together. He was very fond of you. His letter should arrive soon," he added.

I wanted to turn off the sound of his voice. But I couldn't.

"I know this is a shock. He said he hadn't told you of his illness because he didn't want you to worry. That's so typical of Dad."

We carried on talking for a while, but I was numb and could hardly take it all in. He defended Chuck's decision to keep me in the dark about his health. I didn't care. All I wanted to do was curl into a fetal position and stay there forever.

The following day, Chuck's letter arrived. My hands were shaking so much I had to compose myself. The words came in and out of focus as I tried to read it. I sat down on the floor with my back against the wall—my favorite position.

My dearest girl,

By the time you get this, I will have shuffled off this mortal coil. One thing I never told you is that I am—was—a cancer survivor. I thought I had beaten the big C. But during a routine visit to the doctor, they found the cancer had returned and spread. It is stage four and inoperable. I'll spare you the details, but I didn't want you to see me like this.

This happened after your visit, and that's the main reason I didn't pressure you to share your life with me here in Payson.

You brought so much love and happiness to my life. I feel so blessed to have known you. My son, Jonathan, is the executor of my will, and I have asked him to send you those early editions of Mark Twain books you admired—you know, the ones that sat on the shelf above the fireplace. I wish we had more time together, or met sooner.

Do not mourn my passing. Life is a journey, and what's important is the memories we leave behind.

I love you always,

Chuck

My hands were shaking. I was already curled on the floor, sobbing my heart out. I sensed a curtain coming down, as the darkness enveloped me.

***

I don't know how long I remained in that catatonic state. I was vaguely aware that Nick was around, fussing over me. He kept bringing me food and urging me to eat. I guess once a doctor, always a doctor—but my energy and zest for life had gone.

Hari

I returned to work, but even that didn't help with the feelings of sadness and guilt.

The guilt was overpowering. I was tormented with a lot of what-ifs.

What if I hadn't delayed my decision to join him in Payson?

What if he'd told me that he had health issues and was a cancer survivor?

What if we had spent those last few months together?

I felt drained, physically and emotionally. Then Hari called.

"I heard what happened. I'm so, so sorry," she gasped. "Do you want to come to New York? Toby also said we can both go stay with her in LA if we want."

It was so good to hear her voice again.

"I can't take more time off work, but if you're able, why not come and stay with me, here in London?" I said.

"That would be great," she replied without hesitation. "I've dispensed with Ed. The FBI is now dealing with him. I doubt I'll see a penny of the money I sent him. What was I thinking? Emily's boyfriend is moving in with her, so I'm looking to move myself."

It was decided—she'd come to stay with me in London while she weighed up all her options.

She was the tonic I needed. I couldn't wait.

***

Hari

It was a quiet Christmas—not like the one I had planned to have with Chuck—but having Hari there was good for me. She had regained her sparkle and was great company. I was happy to share my home with her. She insisted I put up Christmas decorations and a Christmas tree. She was her old upbeat self.

"I can't afford to buy a house in London anymore," she said one day. "But I've been thinking of buying something—like a small cottage in one of the Home Counties, or even further afield, like Dorset, Devon or Cornwall. The Cotswolds are too expensive and damp. My bones don't like the damp cold weather anymore."

"That's a great idea. I personally like Dorset—closer to London and not as expensive. And don't forget East Anglia too."

"I thought it'd be really neat if I had a cottage in the countryside and you could come and stay weekends…"

I finished the sentence for her. "And you can share my house in London whenever you want to come to town. We can have the best of both worlds—Town and Country."

"It's gonna be okay," said Hari, ever the optimist. She reminded me of our time in Beijing and the many adventures and travels we had with the CCC.

"We were making memories back then. So let's start making some new ones now," she said.

Indeed. Tomorrow is another day—and a new beginning.

The Flasher

"Do you know I was flashed in my first week in Beijing?"

My friend was taken aback.

"What do you mean?" he asked.

So I had to tell him the story of my encounter with the man in the dirty white raincoat.

I arrived in Beijing in early January 2002. It was cold, and the entire city was under a blanket of ice and snow. Mary met me at the airport. She was the sister of the owner of the English language school that had hired me.

I had come to China to teach English as a foreign language. As soon as Beijing got the go-ahead to host the 2008 Olympics, the Chinese Communist government issued a diktat, ordering its citizens to learn English. Everyone working in the tourist industry—taxi drivers, restaurant and hotel staff—was mandated to study English. One does not question the orders of a communist regime. You do as you're told.

Consequently, English language schools mushroomed and flourished, especially in the capital, where the Olympic Games would be held. Some were legitimate, and others were run by less scrupulous entrepreneurs. When you live under an authoritarian regime, circumventing the rules becomes an art form—and often, a way of life. In China, they call it survival.

After the Mao era and the end of the Cultural Revolution, China embarked on the road to recovery. It took several internal coups and Party purges, but the Beijing authorities were determined not to repeat the mistakes of the past. In such a vast country, with the world's largest population, a strong central government was deemed essential. It was the only way to keep the country together—housed, clothed, and fed.

If the Party loosened the reins, it would enable the many centrifugal interests waiting in the background to tear the country apart. It would mean a return to the anarchy of feudalism and warring states.

Under the more moderate and liberal policies of Chou En-lai and Deng Xiaoping, the blue boiler suits of the Mao era were replaced with more colorful, fashionable clothes. The silk, cashmere, and other natural fibers indigenous to China gave a kick-start to the silk, wool, and weaving centers across the country. From an amorphous and uniform grey, China suddenly burst into color, music, and dance.

It wasn't an overnight transformation. It took years and several setbacks. In 1989, the failed attempt at Western-style democracy showed that this awakening could not be hurried. It was two steps forward, one step back.

All these efforts to bring some kind of normalcy to the country—after the excesses of the Mao era—helped make China today the world's second-largest economy. It is confident, powerful, and unafraid to flex its muscles in the global arena. It opened its doors to tourism, foreign investment, and free travel for its people.

The Flasher

A year earlier, I had visited China as a tourist. It was my first trip to the mainland. We visited the silk factories in Suzhou, southeastern China. I watched, enthralled, as the silk cocoons were dipped in boiling water to kill the pupa inside. The hands of the silk workers told their own story. They seemed hard at work and ignored our presence. I think the women were paid by piecework—nothing was going to distract them.

They were probably used to groups of tourists visiting their workplace. I felt like an intruder, but this was my only chance to see how silk was made. The best-quality silk is the one that unravels continuously from its cocoon without breaking. Once it breaks, it is considered of inferior quality, and used to fill mattresses and comforters.

A year later, I returned to China to teach English. Before Beijing, I had lived in Hong Kong for six years. I assumed that, having already experienced Chinese culture, I would adapt quickly to life in the North. After all, I knew how to use chopsticks. I liked Chinese food, culture, art, and people.

But I soon learned that—as in many countries—there is a north-south divide. I realized there was still much to learn and understand about a country with a culture and history stretching back five thousand years.

After settling into my hotel, I decided to explore the surrounding area. I made sure not to wander too far to avoid getting lost. I took the precaution of writing down the name, telephone number, and address of my hotel—just in case I needed to show it to a cab driver.

The Flasher

The sidewalks had been salted and sanded to make them less slippery. Still, I walked carefully. There was a fair amount of traffic and noise, and I took it all in. I was on the verge of a new and exciting adventure.

New smells, sounds, and sights added to my exhilaration. I felt like Alice in Wonderland, and the snow added to the magic.

As I walked along the sidewalk, I sensed I was being followed. I looked back and saw a man in a dirty white raincoat walking rapidly toward me. At the same time, he was muttering something and trying to get my attention by fumbling with the opening of his coat.

I turned away and walked more briskly, hoping to avoid him. I crossed the street. He crossed the street. I took a left turn—so did he. I could feel his breath on the back of my neck.

Oh no! Darn it, I thought. *I've come all this way to China only to meet a flasher in a dirty white coat.*

I remembered some advice I'd heard years earlier: *If you are accosted by a flasher, don't show shock, fear, or embarrassment. That's what they want. Just make some kind of disparaging remark and show you're not impressed.*

Not knowing any Mandarin, I decided my best defense was to laugh in his face. Since I couldn't make a disparaging remark in Chinese, I would try to laugh *disparagingly*—whatever that meant—and show that I was neither embarrassed nor frightened.

I turned to confront him. He was muttering what sounded to me like, "DeeTee, DeeTee."

As I turned, he immediately opened his raincoat.

Inside was a veritable shop of DVDs, and he was saying:

"DVD! DVD! You buy? You buy DVD!"

He was selling DVDs and music CDs. There seemed to be hundreds inside that dirty white raincoat.

I burst out laughing—not with embarrassment, but with sheer relief.

I was thankful it wasn't what I had expected. In retrospect, I don't think I could have managed a disparaging laugh. His purpose was simply to entice me to purchase DVDs and CDs.

I learned later that there is a thriving industry in China in the illegal copying and reproduction of movies and music. The man in the white coat was one of hundreds of sellers I encountered during my time in the country.

They knew the watering holes and eateries foreigners frequented. They would linger in the background, and when the waiters weren't looking, they'd come up to our table to sell their DVDs. If we showed any interest, there was always a fellow co-conspirator lurking nearby—someone wearing a larger raincoat or carrying a bigger bag—who would soon appear with more goods.

They carried American, French, Russian, Chinese, Japanese, British, and Australian movies—both old classics and the latest productions. If they didn't have what you wanted, they'd get it for you. Some even offered to deliver to your home or place of work.

Occasionally, the films would be available even *before* they went on general release in their country of origin. Most of the time, the quality was good, and the price was around US $5–$8. A true bargain.

After I picked up enough Mandarin, I began enjoying the haggling more than the buying. I soon realized there were three different prices in China: one inflated price for foreign tourists, another for expats living and working in China, and the lowest for local Chinese. I always aimed to get a price *below* the local Chinese rate. I became quite good at it.

Many of my Chinese friends wanted to come shopping with me because I was getting lower prices than *they* were.

By the time I left Beijing, I had amassed around 350 DVDs, which I shipped back home. Fortunately, Customs didn't inspect my crated items when I returned to London four years later. I think they would have either confiscated them or fined me—or both.

My years in China were happy ones. Expats, especially those from English-speaking countries, were welcome. From the Chinese government's viewpoint, we were there to enrich the country, help in its growth, and support its rise from the ashes and humiliations inflicted by foreign powers.

The fact that I was from a country that had been part of those humiliations was not held against me.

The Communist government differentiates between relationships among people and relationships between governments. People-to-people friendships are good and encouraged. Government-to-government relations are a different matter.

Beijing was intent on using the Olympic Games to show the world that it had entered the twenty-first century and was well on its way to becoming a global power—a power to be reckoned with. It funneled all its efforts in that direction.

Under the umbrella of communism, capitalism thrived. The incident with the man in the white coat peddling his goods in the streets of Beijing was just one example.

The Party turned a blind eye to these entrepreneurs and hustlers. It encouraged commerce, knowing that as long as people prospered under its regime, they would have no reason to upset the applecart or demand change. Prosperity meant peace.

If the Party turned a blind eye, then the population could turn a blind eye to the Party's control and corruption. It was very much a case of: *"We'll scratch your back, and you'll scratch ours."*

Many of these hustlers were illegal immigrants from the countryside. The Party controlled the number of people allowed to work in the cities. It had quotas for skilled workers. The illegals were always under the threat of being sent back—at best—or imprisoned for hard labor at worst.

Although we were welcome as foreign workers in the big cities, there was still an element of distrust and xenophobia in the countryside and remote parts of China.

There is one instance that comes to mind.

***

During my time in China, I had several visitors. I guess I wasn't the only one who felt the lure of the Far East. I had a Western-style, comfortable apartment with two bedrooms—plenty of space to put people up.

My former colleague from the international school in London, Ruth, came to visit. Her trip coincided with the International Ice and Snow Festival in Harbin, a city in northeastern China, near the Russian border. The China Culture Club was organizing a trip there, and we joined them.

We stayed in Harbin for a couple of nights. Since the sun was shining, Ruth and I decided to take a walk around town. The temperature was minus 15°F—which is normal for that part of the world. Siberia lay just across the border.

We were well bundled up with coats, gloves, warm boots, and several layers under our heavy-duty parkas. I envied Ruth's Russian fur hat with the long ear flaps. My beanie was serviceable, but not as elegant.

The Flasher

Suddenly, I heard Ruth cry out:

"He spat at me! He spat on me!"

"What's going on?" I was a few feet ahead of her and hadn't seen what happened. She pointed to a man standing by the roadside.

"He—*that man*—spat at me!"

Out of nowhere, a crowd gathered around us. The man was still standing there, but now his demeanor had changed—from angry to sheepish, almost frightened.

A young man who spoke English stepped out from the crowd and approached us to apologize. He explained that the cantankerous old man thought we were Russians.

"Why does he dislike Russians? They're your neighbors, just across the border," I asked.

"That's the problem," he replied. "We get many Russian women coming over. They earn money as prostitutes. Some men prefer them to Chinese girls. We don't like it."

"So why does the government allow it?" I asked.

"They don't. But they don't ban it either. It's an illicit business. The women are smuggled across the border. This guy thought you were Russian because of the hat. I'm sorry for what happened."

The young man—clearly a student—looked embarrassed. I thought, *Another example of the Party turning a blind eye to illicit goings-on, as long as the status quo suits its purposes.*

I sensed the crowd also wanted to apologize. They too were embarrassed by the old man's behavior. In many parts of China, one miscreant can bring shame to an entire community.

Despite that incident, the visit to the Ice and Snow Festival was one of the highlights of my time in China. Ruth was good about it. I hope she left with favorable impressions of Cathay and its people.

**

I believe that when one visits or resides in a foreign country, it behooves one to observe the customs and laws of that country. However, there was one occasion when I nearly got arrested in Tiananmen Square, in the center of Beijing.

Tiananmen Square is the largest public square in the world. It has seen many momentous events, from the Red Guard parades during the Cultural Revolution to the failed Democracy Movement of 1989.

It was spring 2002, and while I was showing a friend from Australia around Beijing's famous square, she needed to use the bathroom. I usually avoided going to public toilets in China, but this was an emergency. We'd been walking around for a while and it was a cold day.

We eventually located a public convenience and headed that way. As was the custom at the time, the entrance was guarded by a female toilet paper dispenser. In China, you have to carry your own toilet paper with you when you leave your apartment. Public toilets don't carry toilet paper. Many don't even have hand-washing facilities. In tourist sites, a female will give you some toilet paper she pulls from a toilet paper roll. That's her job.

This female looked rather formidable—stocky, and wearing some kind of uniform. My friend said, "Do you need a uniform to hand out toilet paper?"

It was part question, part joke. The human toilet paper dispenser issued us each one 5x5 inch piece of paper. I politely asked her for more, but she brusquely told me that was all I was getting! We were being rationed!

With icy winds blowing down from the Mongolian steppes, I was not going to argue with this human machine. Without a second thought, I grabbed the roll from her, helped myself to what I felt was my due ration, and did the same for my friend.

The human toilet paper dispenser was furious, cursing us in Chinese. She motioned to a couple of guards nearby, who simply looked away and walked off—reluctant to get involved.

Who wants to mediate between a toilet paper dispenser and a foreigner? Besides, this foreigner could be someone important. A diplomatic incident could ensue. If the Western press got hold of it, they would not pass up the opportunity to write disparaging comments about paper rationing in the country that had invented it.

Can you imagine the headlines?

"Tourist Arrested Over Toilet Paper Issue" or

"Western Bums Require More Toilet Paper."

That's as close as I got to being arrested in China.

When people ask me whether I was frightened or worried about living under a communist regime, I reply that I felt safer walking around the streets of Beijing than in New York or London—especially at night.

Looking back and recalling all the funny and strange encounters I had in China, I feel privileged to have had that opportunity to experience something of its culture.

I saw a nation proud of its ancient civilization and achievements, trying to recreate itself. I watched as the silkworm emerged from its cocoon as a chrysalis, determined to make China great again.

Was that a good or a bad thing?

The question is: good for whom? Bad for whom? Time will tell.

MAGA is not uniquely an American thing. All nations with ancient histories and former empires aim to recreate the past. They want the Empire Phoenix to rise again.

History repeats itself.

Blighty Revisited

(The term "Blighty" emerged during the British Raj in India, where the Urdu word "vilāyatī" meaning "foreign" or "European" was used to describe things or people from Britain.)

After an absence of several years from England, I decided it was time to reacquaint myself with the home country. It'd been a while. Although I had kept in touch with friends and family digitally, I missed the personal touch. I needed to see, face to face, and hug my family. To touch and feel their warmth and love. Skin to skin.

Covid had disrupted many things—work, schools, social activities, and personal encounters. But the greatest disruption of all was the interruption of human non-digital interactions. The remote kind was no substitute. I needed to feel and smell a person's closeness. To "see" their aura up close and personal.

I was also wondering how well my friends had weathered the passage of time. Most probably they were wondering the same thing about me. One friend let me know that she had stopped dyeing her hair and had gone from ginger to white. Her photograph was something of a shock when I saw it, because as long as I knew her, she was a redhead. How much more of a shock a face-to-face encounter would be.

I informed her that I had now been promoted to the "salt and pepper" variety, but refrained from sending her my picture.

An eleven-hour direct flight from San Diego to London got me and my bags there safely. It's strange to feel *dépaysée* in one's own country. It begs the question: "Which is my country?"

The minute I speak to someone in the US, they ask, "Where's your accent from?" My usual answer to this is, "Where the rest of me is from."

Whilst traveling in the UK, and I tell people I'm from the US, they say: "You don't sound American."

Having been an expat for so long, I'm developing an identity crisis. In England, I often have to correct myself and remember to ask for the *loo* and not the *bathroom*; and when I want the first floor in the elevator, to press *G* (sorry—I should have said *lift*).

In Blighty, G stands for the ground floor, which corresponds to the first floor in the US. The first floor for the Brits is the second floor for Americans. Hotels catering to foreign travelers often indicate the first floor with a zero now, but old elevators still use *G* for ground. If you're confused, so am I.

My son is now having his revenge on me. It's his turn to correct me and tell me to express myself in proper English and not Americanisms.

"Mum, it's the High Street, not the Main Street. You're in England now. It's the car park, not the parking lot. It's pronounced *gar-ridge*, not *gahrahge*. Here we walk on pavements, not sidewalks."

This admonition lasted for the duration of my visit. He was right, but I wouldn't admit it. After all, he inherited his stubbornness from me.

When I mentioned the word *GPS* to my friend Denise, she had no idea what I was talking about. In the UK, they refer to their navigation aid as *Sat-Nav,* which stands for satellite navigation.

Churchill was right when he said we were two nations "divided by the same language." I often get confused and mix up the two—American and English.

My first stop in England was Brighton—a lively seaside town in the south. Brits call the southern coast of their country *Costa Geriatrica.* Because of its warm weather and prolonged sunshine, it attracts many retirees. Brighton is the exception. It buzzes with excitement and activities; its pubs and cobbled streets spill over with youth—day trippers, students, and tourists.

Many lanes in the old town have been pedestrianized, thus adding to its charm. I enjoyed sitting outdoors sipping my cup of *joe* and watching the world go by. Occasionally you have to duck as a passing seagull swoops down, dropping his calling card while trying to steal your toast. They're quite fearless, strutting along the promenade, rooftops, and sidewalks, waiting for their chance to exercise their scavenging skills.

I stayed at the Old Ship Hotel, which is on the waterfront. It's what I call "shabby chic." It could do with a fresh coat of paint, and the cleaning leaves something to be desired.

Upon arrival, I was unpleasantly surprised to find that breakfast was not included. They charged fifteen pounds sterling (about $20) extra for each meal. I soon discovered you could get the same breakfast for half that price, just around the corner.

I had been looking forward to my first English breakfast with bangers (English slang for sausages), fried mushrooms, Heinz baked beans, black pudding, tomatoes, and eggs. The picture to the left is an abbreviated version. I was counting calories that day.

The slice of bread was there to mop up the egg yolk and the sauce from the baked beans. Yummy! And look at that bacon! Real ham, not just fat strips fried to a crisp. *Chacun à son goût*—each to his own taste.

On another occasion, a hotel employee started to tell me about the hotel's history and provenance. He thought I was American and wanted to impress me.

It's the oldest hotel in town, believed to have been built in 1559—during the time of horse-drawn carriages. It began life as a tavern and travelers 'inn. It has undergone several renovations since, but the old charm clings to it.

I was more interested in its current sanitary conditions than its provenance. I thanked him for the history lesson and asked if they had ever considered bringing it into the 21st century.

"Oh yes," he replied, without missing a beat. "We now have Wi-Fi and you can book online, which they didn't have in the 16th century."

Touché, I thought.

"And all our rooms are ensuite," he added.

"How did they manage back then when they wanted to go to the bathr…I mean... when they wanted to relieve themselves?" I asked. I nearly used the word *bathroom*.

In England, a bathroom is where you take a bath or have a shower. And Brits don't use the word *restroom*. They rest in the living room, or the den—usually in an armchair. There's nothing restful about sitting on a toilet.

The hotel employee answered, with a twinkle in his eye, "If they wanted to go *tout de suite*, before *ensuite*, there was always the sea."

Silly me. Why didn't I think of that?

That's when I realized what I had missed most about Britain—the wit and dry humor. On the whole, Brits don't take themselves too seriously. We used to call it "gay repartee," but you can't use the word *gay* in its original form today. You can't even say "Gay Paris," as that would have an entirely different connotation.

I wonder how one would translate the ballet *Gaîté Parisienne*, choreographed by Massine in 1938. But I digress. Political correctness is not my forte.

I soon established a good working relationship with the hotel's maintenance department. Perhaps *maintenance department* is too fancy a name for the elderly man who came up to my room three times—once to fix a blocked wash basin, once to fix a wobbly and dangerous toilet seat and the third time to fix a writing table that threatened to lose a leg each time I tried to use it.

By the third time, we were on first-name speaking terms.

My sense of humor enabled me to deal with the wobbly toilet seat, which threatened to send me crashing to the floor in mid-flow. It caused me some anxiety every time I had to use it. While Roger, the maintenance guy, fixed the seat, he told me that his grandson was about to graduate from Sussex University and his daughter was expecting her third child. He was kept busy at his job, he said, as it was an old hotel and needed his constant attention. He could not see himself retiring.

"It's an antique, just like meself," he chuckled. "I've been 'ere over twenty years. I can't retire. I wouldn't know what to do with meself. I think me wife would rather 'ave me out of the house than under her feet all day."

Despite its shabby chic condition, the hotel was full. I guess they had a good PR agent—like a clever realtor who'll place a piece of furniture over that burnt hole in the carpet before taking his pictures. The pictures I saw did not show the dust, the low water pressure, or the faded wallpaper that was coming apart at the seams. The price was right, so I booked it before I got there.

It certainly had character and a certain charm that appealed to American visitors who consider anything more than 70 years old a valuable antique.

The elevator was one example. As I squeezed into this tiny antique, a fellow passenger started talking to me. I couldn't understand a word she was saying. I asked her where she was from.

"Daaaahrbishaahr," she replied.

I smiled and thanked her. Derbyshire is a county in the East Midlands. I had expected her to tell me she came from some exotic foreign country or some remote island off the coast of Ireland or Scotland, where they spoke only Gaelic. She had a very thick accent, and I wondered whether all Derbyshire people sounded like her. I had forgotten about English regional accents. I'd been away too long.

A ride in that particular elevator was quite scary. It screeched and sounded as if it was on its last legs. The management was aware of the fear this caused to its passengers. To reassure us, they placed a notice next to the elevator on the ground floor:

> *This lift was installed in 1920*
> *(Maintained on a regular basis)*
> *It's a little slower compared to modern lifts.*
> *It will be at your service as soon as possible.*
> *Thank you for your patience.*

It wasn't my patience that was tried, but my fear that we might be plunged to death in this tiny square box. My room was on the 5th floor and my knees refused to climb the stairs. That piece of early 20th-century mechanical history was my only means of going up and down. At my age, abseiling was out of the question. Each time I had to use it, I hoped and prayed it had been recently serviced. The word *"regularly"* didn't cut it with me.

Inside it said: *"Room for six,"* but two average-sized Americans, or one obese person, or myself with all my luggage, filled it to capacity.

The day I checked out, I summoned it to my floor. I squeezed in and began my descent. It stopped on the 3rd floor. An elderly Chinese couple had been waiting patiently to go down for breakfast. The door opened, and they saw me with all my bags, shook their heads, sighed, then waved me on.

Blighty Revisited

I love Brighton for its history and its *joie de vivre*. On my last day, I took a promenade on the pier to say goodbye to the town and send good wishes and prayers to my home across the Pond. There was a small funfair at the end of the pier, and I took a ride on it. I posted a picture of me on the merry-go-round on FB—just for the fun of it.

Then it was "goodbye Brighton" as I boarded the train for London for another adventure. This time I made sure breakfast was included in the hotel price.

*** *

I was becoming quite good at making train, bus, and hotel reservations online. Booking my train ticket from Brighton to London, the bot obligingly offered me a list of preferences from its drop-down menu. It included the wine and food lists from the restaurant car. I chose a window seat close to the baggage rack. That way I could keep an eye on my bags.

I hadn't ridden a train since my last visit to the UK, which was many years ago. I love train journeys. As a child, I had crisscrossed Europe several times, and the excitement of being on a train remains with me to this day. The gentle roll and occasional whistle blow envelop me with a sense of peace. Someone else is doing the driving, and I can sit back and relax—think my thoughts and even nod off.

Most train stations in the UK date from the days of the Industrial Revolution when iron and steel became readily available with cheap labor. Many are built as grand architectural palaces and have a following of historians and fans who study their history. Most were built when the steam engine was invented. Other European countries, too, boast beautiful railway stations. The one that comes to mind is the one in Antwerp, Belgium, dubbed *"The Railway Cathedral."* It is truly beautiful.

Until New Zealand took the crown, Britain had the longest-named train station in the world. It was in Wales and boasted fifty-eight letters to its name—in Welsh, of course:

Llanfairpwllgwyngyllgogerychwyrndrobwllllantysiliogogogoch   is now the second-longest train station name in the world.

This crazy name didn't come about by chance. The town name was contrived in 1869 as a publicity stunt to give the station the longest name in Britain.

When I was a kid, we tried to memorize it and use it as a tongue twister. I could never get it right, however hard I tried.

Contrary to what some Americans think, Britain is not an egalitarian or socialist country. Our trains have a two-class passenger system—standard and first class. The seats in first class have more space, extra legroom, and are generally wider than the standard class seats. The carriages are quieter, calmer, and more comfortable than the standard class. Ticket inspectors walk through the carriages to check your ticket and ensure that the commoners do not sneak into the first-class compartment. I tried it once.

It was during my daily commute, a fifty-minute train journey. It had been a hard day at work; I was tired. When I boarded the train for my homebound journey, there were no seats in the standard compartments. I sneaked into first class and sat down. The ticket inspector informed me that I was in the wrong carriage. I tried to explain that I wasn't feeling well, but he unceremoniously booted me out and accompanied me to the proletariat section, where I stood for the rest of my journey. I never tried to cheat again. Usually, I could find a seat, and I was thankful I lived in a country that had one of the best railway systems in the world. Until Maggie Thatcher changed things. But that's another story for another time.

Trainspotting is a popular pastime in the UK. Individuals or groups get together to observe trains and their particular characteristics. Many people see trainspotting as a niche hobby, similar to birdwatching or stamp collecting. I could never understand it, but I enjoyed the eponymous movie that came out in 1996. It introduced the American public to a very British hobby and the antics of train enthusiasts. Personally, I prefer visiting railway stations to standing on windy railroad banks waiting for trains to come by.

Technology has invaded these old stations. It's an unavoidable intrusion. Neon-lit arrival and departure signs, automatic ticket-dispensing machines, and gates that respond to the touch of a cellphone coexist with Victorian elegance and strength. I think this invasion is ugly. It distracts from the elegance and beauty of the building. Many of the stations have survived wars and were built to last. Brighton train station was no exception. It was built in 1840. Its high dome ceiling is made of glass and steel, rising above the notice boards and ETA signs. It has a look of Victorian sturdiness. Early train stations had high ceilings to allow the steam to escape and not suffocate the passengers.

For long journeys, there are compartments with couchettes, velvet-lined walls and curtains, and a restaurant car that, at times, can rival a Michelin-star eatery. The longest single train journey in Britain is one that starts in Aberdeen, Scotland and ends in Penzance, Cornwall. A mere 722 miles.

One tap of my cellphone opened the gate for me and my luggage to get onto the platform. I was on my way to London, but somewhat sad to be leaving Brighton. I would miss the sea air and sunsets over the ocean.

As I settled in my seat, I noticed several USB ports spread like acne, embedded along the aisles. Earlier on, I had noticed that buses too were beset with this infestation. The law of supply and demand has produced a slew of furniture with USB ports—such as sofas, armchairs, lamps, bedside tables—and even beds.

Capitalism encourages us to buy, buy, buy—out with the old, in with the new. Advertisers are adept at making you feel deprived if you don't have the latest, biggest, and most expensive gizmo. I guess people carriers such as planes, trains, and buses feel the urge to cater to their passengers 'new addiction—their need to remain connected to their cellphones. If their phones run out of juice, they might become violent. Withdrawal symptoms? Who knows?

When Covid was at its height, many companies refused to take cash and would only deal with credit or debit cards. Since the details of one's credit card can be downloaded onto one's phone, the mobile phone has replaced the need to carry a credit card—fast replacing the need to carry plastic. With one tap you can pay your bills, open doors to theaters and restaurants, and make purchases both on and offline. Tap, tap, tap and your money leaves your bank account. One tap and you get doors open to the theater, the movies, and the restaurant— another tap and you pay your bill—any bill, from your airfare to your hotel to your boarding pass.

It's easy to overspend as you do not actually see the money and handling it. If you don't see it and count it in your hands, you can go overboard. Before you know it, your credit balance becomes a debit one. You go from black to red in no time.

***

When a baby is born, the umbilical is cut off and discarded with the placenta. All that remains is the belly button. Since mankind seems unable to disengage itself from this new umbilical—the cellphone—companies pander to their passengers 'needs and supply them with the means to stay plugged in. It's ironic that something that's meant to keep us connected isolates and disengages us from our immediate surroundings. You don't have to engage with another human. Simply pay by credit or debit card and that's it.

Despite my misgivings, cellphones do have their uses. In some cases, they make our lives more manageable. When you think of all the information they carry and the speed with which we can connect to people, information, maps, and make reservations, it's priceless. Some of my contemporaries wish things hadn't changed so much. Nostalgia is their comfort zone—a place to linger and vent. But change is a constant, and much as we'd like to, we can't put the clock back.

All these thoughts danced in my head on my way to London, in sync with the train's movement. I watched as people got on and off at various stops—most of them clutching that ubiquitous little piece of plastic to their ear. Along the route, my eyes were drawn to the beautiful countryside, with its green undulating hills, dotted with pastures, horses, cows, sheep, and hamlets. I wondered how long it would be before these idyllic places would be marred by tall posts carrying electronic cables, wind turbines, or telephone towers. All done in the name of "progress."

My reverie was interrupted by the woman seated across from me. She was having a loud, personal conversation on her phone. She was upset about something. She made us all unwilling participants in her woes. This did not alter my previous unkind thoughts about cellphones. I was so tempted to butt in and join in her conversation. *Really, he did that? He actually said that? Well... if I were you I'd... Can you dial down the volume, please? We don't need to hear that! Lady, watch your language, there are children on board.* But I didn't. I did what everyone else did—pretended I wasn't listening while I seethed with frustration.

"We shall soon be arriving at Victoria," boomed the loudspeaker. That was my stop. Time to gather my bags and make sure I had everything with me.

I was going to travel around the UK for about two months. I came prepared with a big suitcase, which I checked in, a carry-on, a backpack, and a small purse. With so much luggage, getting on and off trains, in and out of cabs, took some planning. Thank God for kind people. It was the kindness of strangers that helped me navigate around England, including the London Underground, escalators, buses, and overhead railway bridges.

I put it down to my grey hair. I guess people take pity on a granny struggling with a ton of luggage. Many times a total stranger, male or female, offered to carry one or two of my bags. They were angels sent to help me on my travels. Their help was most welcome and much appreciated. I also learned to pick stations with elevators, escalators, and taxi ranks. It's no fun waiting for an Uber in drizzling rain. Small provincial stations were a problem. That's when I'd call a friend to come and pick me up—one advantage of having friends with cars—whom I also consider angels, and much appreciated.

From Victoria Station, the cab took me to my hotel in High Street Kensington, which is a part of London I know well. Part of my old stomping grounds and close to where my former house was. Checking in was a breeze since everything had been booked online. The elevators were plentiful and roomy. I did not have to listen to the groans and jerky movements of the antique contraption that passed for an elevator at the Brighton shabby-chic hotel. I missed it. It certainly had character.

My London hotel was comfortable, with modern elevators, a good-sized room, and good water pressure. Not shabby chic, but modern chic. Breakfast was included in the price. I did not have to summon the maintenance department for repairs. I looked forward to seeing my two London cousins and meeting up with old friends. I gave myself a couple of days to explore on my own and reacquaint myself with the London I loved and missed. I've always said that I am a city girl. I enjoy brief stays in the countryside but always return to the city, happy to be back. My home is in the city, and the city is home to me.

It had been a few years since I visited the UK, but as I emerged from my hotel the next morning, I wasn't prepared for the changes I found.

Blighty Revisited

The saying "never go back to a place where you've been happy" was beginning to take shape in my mind, where I had stored fond memories of my former home and the area. Those fond memories were now being jostled and marred by this new "normal" that was attacking my senses. I remembered my first holiday job, shopping in fashion boutiques and department stores, and going to Holland Park, which was at the top end of Kensington High Street. My cousin Nick and I had attended several operas there during their summer season. Those were my memories. The department stores, the familiar shops, and restaurants had gone. Vanished. Disappeared. Replaced by shops selling cellphones, Starbucks, and McDonald's.

What I encountered, after all these years, was a different world. A world of heavy traffic, car exhaust fumes, noise, overcrowded sidewalks, pollution, and people walking while talking on their cellphones, unaware of those around them. I had to duck, turn, get off the sidewalk, and nearly got run over in my efforts to stop being knocked down by these individuals. They were like robots attached to their mobile phones, which made them less mobile and more like bulldozers, ploughing their way through this sea of humanity. Who were these people? Where had they come from? Most of the people seemed to be from South Asia.

Having ruled over a vast empire, Britain had always had immigrants. They tended to stay together in enclaves. But these newcomers were not your run-of-the-mill asylum seekers or immigrants. They were well-dressed and confident. They carried shopping bags from expensive, prestigious departments. Where have all the white Anglo-Saxons gone? I wondered. London's ethnography had changed.

I knew that curry scored the highest rate of take-out orders in the UK. Chinese food came a close second, with the traditional fish and chips lagging behind. The bland fare of meat, veg, and potatoes had been replaced by more exotic dishes. Britain was being colonized by the people and food of its former colonies. I tried to analyze my feelings and reactions to this change. On the one hand, I felt it was good. We should not fear change. But not all change is good. I thought of how the arrival of hordes of white immigrants from Europe had altered Native American culture and Native Americans became an endangered species. Were the native Brits becoming an endangered species? I decided that fear of change and fear of the "other" is not healthy or safe.

I was on a visit to see family, and friends, chew the cud—as Brits say——with them and reminisce. I'd be adding stories to my vast collection of memories and passing them on to anyone willing to listen.

As for the changes I noticed during my visit, I can only echo my friend Fran: "That's life. It is what it is."

Moving On

Did you know I have two PhDs? One in Procrastination and a second in Prevarication. Most of my peers are equally well-qualified. We sing from the same hymn book: "One day," "When I have time," "When I'm feeling better," "When I retire," and "Eventually, I'll get round to it." I was once given a round wooden tray with the words *Round Tuite* engraved on it. John, my husband, often maintained that I should do something about *my* stuff. He's the tidy and organized one. It was always *my* stuff. Never *our* stuff.

My *mañana* attitude about our accumulated stuff came to an abrupt end when we had to make a life-changing decision—relocate to another state—a change necessitated primarily for health reasons and a desire to improve our lifestyle. It was no longer a case of me doing something about *my* stuff but dealing with both his and mine. We now have a different tune buzzing around: "Time's up," "Hurry up," "Get started with the packing," and the most persistent of all: "The U-Haul's coming soon."

Though he'd never admit it, my other half can be a bit of a hoarder too, albeit a tidy and organized one, unlike me. When I can't find something—anything—I ask: "Honey, have you seen that set of knitting needles lately?" or, "Where did I put that Pyrex platter we used last Christmas?" And, in most cases, he can find it. Whereas I hate being organized or tidy. Because when I do, then I can't find anything. I attribute this to being an artist. Only half of my brain works—the right brain. At least that's my explanation—or excuse. Take your pick. It's no brainer.

When we decided to relocate, we had no choice but to downsize as well. We were exchanging a four-bedroom adobe home that had half an acre of yard in New Mexico for a 1,200-square-foot clapboard craftsman cottage in California. We outbid seven other wannabe buyers, and I couldn't wait to make it to our new home. John kept saying that we needed several months to pack and leave. But when I pointed out that we couldn't afford to pay taxes and insurance premiums on two properties, he too realized that speed was of the essence.

Once we started down that road—which had a very steep learning curve—we began picking up soundbites of advice from others who had preceded us along this path. A friend who had moved several times between states informed us that we were joining the ranks of people who were also downsizing—the Boomers (1946–1964) and the Silent Generation (1928–1945). They too were getting rid of stuff.

The Silent Generation endured the Great Depression and WWII. For this reason, they saved everything. They called it thrift—saving for a rainy day—perhaps anticipating another depression. My mother's favorite quote, "Waste not, want not," is still ingrained in me. I have been known to save rubber bands, plastic bags, cardboard boxes (sorry, Amazon), empty jars, threadbare towels, old magazines, newspapers, and books—just to name a few. You never know when they might come in handy. Nowadays we call it hoarding.

Moving On

Baby Boomers were caught in the recession of 2008. After years of being told to spend, spend, spend, and use their plastic—because it takes the waiting out of wanting—they saw their savings, pension funds, and homes devalue, and their purchasing power diminished. They too are downsizing. As a result, flea markets, Goodwill stores, and thrift shops are thriving. Every time I go there, they seem well-stocked. One of our newly married granddaughters furnished her first home, very stylishly, with furniture from various dumpsters and thrift stores. I found comfort in the thought that I might be able to palm off some of our stuff to family and friends. But I was disappointed when this did not happen.

It was not that easy to give away, donate, or sell "stuff" because the market of supply and demand had gone bust. Plenty of supply but no demand. Our move came at a bad time. It hurts when you part with something you thought was valuable or precious to you, and your nearest and dearest don't want it. The current generation was not interested in collecting memorabilia. At least, not *our* memorabilia. My son turned down a valuable sterling silver cutlery set because, as he put it, "Mum, we can't be bothered to polish something that we'll hardly ever use." And to add insult to injury, he added, "It won't go in the dishwasher. We'll have to wash it by hand."

In the meantime, we had to decide what to leave and what to take with us. And who decides? John finally realized that he couldn't read every letter exchanged between his parents and grandparents in the early years of the 20th century, under the pretext that he was sorting them out. Neither could we keep every memento and photograph collected over decades.

For years, our two-car garage had not embraced a single vehicle in its bosom. Cars are parked on the driveway, and we drive them on the parkway. I believed that once things were stored in the garage—out of sight—they'd stay there until needed. But out of sight meant also out of mind, because when we started with the garage, it was like a nightmare that had come to haunt us. The shelves buckled under the weight of rows and rows of photograph albums and other discarded items, as well as boxes marked "Christmas," "Thanksgiving," "Fall Décor," and toys for children and grandchildren who had outgrown them years ago. Then we had my husband's workbench, tools, wood splitter, rotary saw, a couple of bicycles (some with and some without wheels), and several broken kitchen gadgets waiting to be "fixed" by my husband, Mr. Fix-it. They had to go—no room for them in our new home.

Blended families work under different dynamics. Ours is a blended family. I did not want to be the "wicked stepmother" who threw out their pictures and memories. Their late mother had captured every facet of their growing up in those albums. They belonged to them. When we asked them to come and take them away, we realized we'd made a big mistake. They dutifully came and picked a handful of photos—perhaps nine or ten pictures, not albums. They spent some time looking at them, rekindling memories, and giggling. We tried: "Are you sure you don't want that picture of yourself blowing out your candles?" or, "How about this one, taken three minutes after you blew out those candles?" We got no bites. They went to the local recycling site.

I suspect the habit of making memories, spending hours sticking photos into albums, and labeling everything with place, time, and date, is more for the benefit of the parents than the children. Nowadays, social media is used by many as a repository of "happy" times. The immediacy of social media leaves no time for a leisurely perusal of ancestral photo albums. Have you noticed that everyone on Facebook these days has to look deliriously happy? Or pretend to be. Of course, social media provides an immediate and wider audience. Besides, albums—like books—take up space and gather dust. Once the kids leave home, the parents are left with the memories and the stuff.

The photo albums went to the dump, along with many other items. We had told them this would happen if they didn't take them.

Meanwhile, the clearing out continued. What to do with those huge portraits of ancestors, also stowed away—the portraits, not the ancestors—in the garage. No smiles there. Painted by well-known artists of the time, and wearing their Sunday best, they seemed to look down on us, as if disapproving. Well, who wouldn't if you stuck them in the garage and left them there to gather dust? If they knew that they were destined for the estate sale, they'd frown even more.

Somewhere in another box, I found all my notes from college. All those pearls of wisdom dripping from the lips of my tutors. Why did I keep them? What about those newspaper cuttings of articles, news, and views, now so obsolete and passé? Tempted as I was to read them—you never know, there might be something worth keeping there—I hardened my heart and trashed them. I think going over and re-reading old letters and notes is a kind of emotional self-gratification—perhaps amid all the upheaval I was searching for some sort of justification for having kept them.

***

The capitalist system works on supply and demand and the continual cycle of buying and selling. They sell and we buy. So we fill our homes until we cannot put any more "stuff" in them. The overflow goes in the shed, the garage, the attic, and anywhere we can find room. I know people who resorted to renting a storage unit.

Our family and friends were surprised when we became a one-car household just before our move. Instead of praise for reducing our carbon footprint, we got: "But don't you need your car?" and "How can you manage?" They were almost commiserating the "loss" of our truck and second vehicle, waiting to see how long we'd last without them.

They're still waiting.

The car is not a luxury, but essential. With an underfunded and poor public transport system, the private car is a necessity. But for two retired "wrinklies," running two cars plus a truck was not.

Persuading my husband to part with his car was easy. But when it came to his truck, he resisted. Coming from London, I saw the truck as a workman's vehicle—to be used on farms in the countryside, covered in mud, and left to rust outside. Before I came to the U.S., when a guy referred to his pick-up in gushing epithets, I assumed he was referring to a hooker he had picked up or his current squeeze. I hadn't realized the symbiotic relationship between a man and his truck.

John's truck already had over 200,000 miles to its credit. It sat parked under a shedding pine tree. Next to it lay a makeshift trailer, covered in war wounds from years of service. The two went hand in glove together. They were a couple, and even when uncoupled, the car and the trailer lay side by side in the front drive. They had served us well over the years; now they were past their use-by date and had to be retired.

I came from London to the American Southwest. It was quite a culture shock. On several occasions, my ignorance of Americanisms and unfamiliarity with American accents caused misunderstandings. When John and I went house-hunting for our first home, I accused him of being vulgar.

"What are you talking about?" he said.

"You asked the owner if he had a raving hooker!" I yelled at him. "What were you thinking?"

"I never said such a thing."

"Yes, you did. When we were walking by the side of the house, you looked at the space next to the garage and asked if they had a raving hooker!"

He burst out laughing.

"It's not funny." I was fuming.

After he composed himself, he said: "I asked if they had an RV hook-up."

Ten years later, we were to leave that house—which incidentally didn't have an RV hookup—for the Golden State. After much deliberation, John eventually sold his beloved truck back to Toyota. As we handed the keys to the salesman, I could read the salesman's mind: *Baby, welcome back to Daddy!*

Letting go of the truck and cars was only the beginning of our relocation woes. One of the first things we needed to get was boxes. You can't relocate without boxes. Trying to be frugal and remembering my mother's "Waste not, want not" aphorism, we delved into the trash areas at McDonald's and Wendy's to find them——not a pleasant task. Soon we realized that the boxes came with the lingering odors of hamburgers and french fries. We gave in and bought new ones. Each time we had to fork out more money for something unplanned, we told ourselves it was a necessary expense. This included rolls of two-inch-wide packing tape and three tape dispensers. In the meantime, the packing, taping, and stress continued.

Ah, the tape. That's where things started to unravel. The tape and its dispenser became my nemesis. I could never find a dispenser when I needed one. Our stress level on the Richter scale met new heights. Add to that the need to downsize in a hurry, and you have a lethal cocktail of exhaustion, frustration, anger, and regrets. No wonder most people delay and make all kinds of excuses when it comes to downsizing. I too kept putting it off, but now we had no choice. We had to deal with all that stuff.

Under stress, paranoia set in. I imagined the tape and its dispenser were trying to prevent us from leaving—convinced that both of them were in cahoots to make my life a misery. Several times the dispenser spat out the tape so that it could attach itself to anything and everything other than the intended object. Even our dog, Maisie, got a dose. Removing the tape from a shaggy Old English Sheepdog is as difficult as removing chewing gum from a child's hair. Of course, Maisie the dog was coming to California with us, but not bubble-wrapped. At night, I lay in bed, peeling tiny bits of tape off my body and clothes. And when asleep, I had a recurring nightmare of a dog growling viciously at me with teeth like those of the dispenser—the very one that kept drawing blood during the day. The worst trick of all was when the tape decided to go on strike and shut down completely—hermetically sealed, causing me to waste precious minutes trying to find its starting point.

We tried to organize ourselves and simplify the mammoth task we faced before us. We labeled several trash bags and boxes—Donations, Estate Sale, Goodwill, Trash. Did I say "simplify"? This caused even more trouble. John and I couldn't agree on what went where. Should the never-used third meat carving set go to Donations or the Estate Sale?

"It was my Aunt Betty's wedding gift to us," he said.

"Yes, I know, but we never used it. Look, it's still in its original box with her card in it."

The man who kept urging me to sort out *my* stuff wouldn't part with his thermal underwear.

"But honey, sweetie," I said, trying to sweeten the pill, "we're going to Southern California. You don't need thermal underwear there."

"It might come in handy," was his frequent response when I questioned his decisions.

Not to be undone, I responded the same way when I was being challenged to part with a second coffee maker, rusty metal cake tins, my collection of mugs from around the world, and numerous kitchen gadgets. This exchange between John and me was repeated with every single closet, cupboard, and piece of furniture. Eventually, with time pressing on mercilessly, we labeled one bag TBD—to be decided.

I fess up: I love kitchen gadgets and have far too many. Every time we went to a state fair or saw a demo on TV, I'd fall for the sales pitch. Hobbies and special interests were magnets for stuff. In my case it was painting; in John's case it was weaving. Over the years, we accumulated art books, canvases, brushes and paints, several floor looms, cones of yarn, and other weaving paraphernalia. We both considered our hobbies and all that went with them indispensable—a common trait of hobbyists, collectors, and crafters. We often define ourselves by our hobbies. "What do you do?" and the answer would be: "I'm a painter," or "I'm a sculptor."

Both John and I love books. We had so many that we could have started our very own lending library. The local senior center received most of them, but finally, they too could not handle the deluge and asked us to stop. The same with the two local libraries, which eventually refused our donations because they ran out of space. I'm ashamed to say that a few ended up in the trash. If we could have taken everything with us, we would have. I too had fallen into the trap of obeying that subliminal voice urging us to: buy, buy, buy.

"Waste not, want not. Want not." And "Think how that money could have been put to better use." My mother's ghost was waving an accusatory finger. Guilt and remorse were now added to our stress factor.

I had heard stories about family members having to clear out the homes of relatives who had died. In one case, three dumpsters were rented and everything was tossed in them. The dearly departed had been a hoarder. Her executors found stacks of stuff, some still in its original packaging. The progeny were interested in the proceeds from the sale of her house, not its contents. At least in our case, we separated the good, the bad, and the ugly and found ways of disposing of them. Big items and anything that was not given away or thrown out were destined for the estate sale.

We asked a couple of estate sales companies to give us a quote for the disposal of some very fine furniture, carpets, silver, and antiques. Most charged fifty percent. One agent came to our home, looked around, made notes, and turned up her nose. As if our stuff was of no interest to her, hardly worth her while—by taking half the proceeds, she was doing us a favor. With one week to go, we had no choice. We chose a company that charged only thirty percent.

You might wonder why we did not hire a firm to move us lock, stock, and barrel. Several reasons: financial (it would be too expensive), and lock, stock, and barrel from a 3,000-square-foot home would hardly fit into a 1,200-square-foot house. Sadly, we were the only ones who could decide what to take and what to leave. The sorting took time. It was also heart-wrenching. Each item had a story to tell.

Another factor needed to be considered: our adobe home with its kiva fireplaces belonged very much to the Southwest, to New Mexico. Our furniture and décor reflected this style. I couldn't envision them in our new small craftsman bungalow in San Diego. They'd look out of place. Perhaps there was a hint also of "out with the old and in with the new." There's something exciting in buying new furniture and décor for a new home.

***

Downsizing is more than just a physical activity. Easier from the outside looking in. I have no problem telling others what and how to downsize. But, when the shoe's on my foot, it's a different story. I think downsizing requires a mega mindset shift. For years, our economic system had encouraged me to buy, acquire, and amass a stock of items that apparently I "needed."

Remember the little ditty when we were encouraged to use plastic? *It takes the waiting out of wanting.* Not only that but I was fed the lie that by engaging in a lot of retail therapy, I was helping the economy. Yay! That's real patriotism for you. As my hard-earned money left my bank account, I was keeping the cogwheels of capitalism oiled and running.

I was born and lived in cities all my life. I never understood people who chose to live on top of mountains or out in the boonies. Mother Nature is best admired from a car window, a train, or the TV screen. I like to step out of my front door and see people, traffic, and the world rushing by, with shops around the corner.

When I came to America, I met people who chose to live off the grid. I was surprised to see how contented, productive, and happy they were. They were normal people in tune with nature, and I envied their frugal lifestyle.

My friend Valerie is a true minimalist. Her house exudes not only elegance but an aura of peace and harmony. She told me she had only one dinner service for four.

"You mean you have only four plates, bowls, knives, forks, spoons? How do you manage?" I asked.

She simply smiled and assured me that she managed perfectly well. When we visited Taiwan, she was not the one rushing into tourist shops buying souvenirs and knick-knacks. Her small carry-on case got lighter as we traveled.

"How come?" I asked her.

"Oh, I brought old clothes with me, and after I use them, I just leave them behind for the hotel staff," she replied. "I don't need them. I've got more than enough clothes."

I was impressed with her attitude and indifference to the siren calls of shopkeepers and tour guides.

Admirable as I thought living off the grid was, my mind was finding many excuses and reasons why it wasn't for us: It's for younger people. We can't move away from family and friends. We love where we are now. Perhaps if we were twenty years younger.

Episodic pangs of remorse over the need to reduce my carbon footprint, avoid waste, and simplify our lifestyle were swept aside and placed on the back burner: *mañana*. Until, ultimately, there was no back burner anymore, but a U-Haul with its mouth wide open was sitting in our front drive. The clock was ticking. We had reached the eleventh hour.

Darn tape and dispenser! Any more trouble from you, and you'll wind up in the fireplace—I'll light the match myself.

***

In the midst of all the chaos caused by our move, I was guilt-ridden. Guilt not because we were getting rid of things, but because I realized we had too much. Seeing the amount of stuff emerging from closets, drawers, cupboards, the shed, garage, and attic filled me with shame.

Moving On

Guilt and shame are heaped on us by those who manipulate us—advertisers, marketers, promoters, and company PRs. The pressure to consume grows during every public holiday and festive season. They know how to push our buttons and send those subliminal messages. They appeal to our greed, our need to impress, our love interests, and a variety of other emotions, so that we will part with our money. Accumulating and hoarding have now become a way of life. Alvin Toffler foresaw this in his 1970 book *Future Shock*. He coined the phrase "built-in obsolescence" as a warning. We refused to listen.

Messages and ads make us feel guilty and ashamed if we don't buy a dozen red roses or expensive chocolates for our significant other on Valentine's Day. We are made to feel inadequate if our home is not as beautiful as those showcased on TV, and if our car still carries the dings and scars of previous owners—no longer second or third-hand, but "pre-owned" —as if second-hand implies inferior. About forty percent of American households buy a new car every year—then we complain about congestion and pollution.

I noticed that people who frequently enjoyed my hospitality seldom returned the compliment. Reciprocity apparently never entered their minds. My late mother-in-law had her own explanation for this: *It's breeding, my dear. No breeding.* It sounds snobbish, but there may be some truth to it. I think the real reason they do not invite people to their homes is because they feel their homes are not fancy enough, or they lack the skills to entertain. It's a form of laziness and bad manners. It's always easier to accept an invitation than to offer one.

A friend once said to me: "Before I can invite anyone for dinner, I'd have to downsize big time and get a cleaning crew in." Just as she was about to tackle her stuff, she inherited her deceased brother's hoard. Now, while the late owner rests in his grave, his possessions rest—at great expense—in rented storage units.

I felt sorry for her. Then I realized that I too, could fall into the same trap. Facing relocation and downsizing got me thinking about how I wanted to live the rest of my life.

***

The desire to reduce my carbon footprint was gradual. I must admit that when futurists like Toffler and Al Gore came on the scene, I was too selfish and lazy to take heed. Like an ostrich, I buried my head in the sand. Until the tsunami of climate change data gave me the jolt I needed. Change started with me—from within.

In the last forty-plus years, there has been increasing awareness and proof that human behavior threatens our planet. The delicate balance between humans and nature is constantly being upended by greed, selfishness, and indifference. There is a growing awareness among the young about the dangers which we and previous generations have created. We owe it to them to leave them a planet where they can live and breathe freely, without becoming an endangered species.

Globalization has highlighted our interdependence. Living off the grid is no longer the domain of religious groups like the horse-and-buggy Amish and Mennonites, or a few eccentrics. Other groups such as the tiny house movement, earthships (which were first built in the arid climate of New Mexico), straw-bale homes, and the use of recycled materials in construction are gaining momentum. The younger generation is espousing these efforts to reduce waste and realizes the need for recycling. But there's still more work to be done. A lot more people to convince.

Getting rid of junk has become more than just a personal issue. For years, developed nations have dumped their junk in third-world countries—now renamed "developing countries." Our reach for the stars has filled space with debris that can endanger future space travel. We have polluted our seas to such an extent that sea creatures are suffering. We have a Herculean task before us to educate and inform ourselves and others on how best to reduce waste and dispose of trash in order to protect our environment.

I realized that the best way is to start with ourselves—in our own homes. I was aided and abetted in my efforts by several advocates of a simpler lifestyle on social media, YouTube, and books. They became my go-to helpers and mentors. They gave me the impetus I needed to downsize big time and change my lifestyle—actually, *our* lifestyle, since we are a couple.

The cynic in me recognizes that these gurus advocating a simpler lifestyle are also making money with their preaching. They saw a niche in the market. But I also realize that I have a choice: to spend my money on "stuff" I don't need, or on advice on reducing my stash. The choice is mine, and I'm grateful that I have that choice.

Changing one's mindset is the first step up to what can be an arduous climb. But once you get to the top—oh my—the view and the feeling of achievement are worth the effort. We were the only ones who could make that change and the only ones to see it through. In other words, we now controlled the stuff, instead of the stuff controlling us. John was supportive and together we speedily worked to meet the deadline for our move.

***

Our relocation and downsizing took place several years ago. We now live in Southern California enjoying life in our small craftsman home. As I bask in the sun, I watch the hummingbirds and butterflies in our backyard and think: *It's time to declutter once again!*

We are not hoarders, but we soon realized that we did not get rid of enough stuff when we relocated. Our hobbies soon filled our three-car garage. Our one family car is parked outside. There is also the great temptation coming from the many wonderful thrift stores in the area. Who can resist a bargain, especially when you're told you're saving money?

Yes, it's time to think about downsizing again. Another estate sale? I'm thinking about it.

The Night Caller

Vicky was sound asleep when she woke up suddenly. It wasn't the regular post-midnight call to the bathroom. Her bladder wasn't screaming. Something else woke her up. *Am I going crazy?* she thought. *I'm beginning to imagine things—hear things that go bump in the night.* She looked at her bedside clock. It was one after midnight. She was about to turn and go back to sleep when she heard it again.

***

For Vicky, it had been another exhausting day. She had settled Carl, her invalid husband, for the night. It was the regular pattern: place a glass of water by his bedside, his phone handy (just in case he needed it), his hearing aids placed in their charger, and his dentures soaking overnight in the dental solution. She gave him his cough mixture and morphine dimmed the light, and wished him good night.

The change had come upon them unexpectedly. Vicky married late in life—she was in her late forties. Carl was fifteen years ahead of her. He was strong, healthy, and active. She called him "Mister Fix-It," because he loved nothing better than doing projects around the house. "The moment the words are out of my mouth, he'd be there fixing it," she said. "He'll even fix breakfast for me."

It was her sense of humor that helped her navigate this new chapter in their lives. When the diagnosis came that Carl suffered from an incurable lung disease, their world was turned upside down. It pained her to see

215

her previously strong, independent man become fearful and emotionally needy. Always a solitary figure, he went into deep depression and stayed glued to the living room sofa, refusing to leave the house or see anyone. His lung specialist told him that if he contracted Covid he wouldn't survive, which added to his fear and isolation.

When he developed bedsores and his legs had atrophied after months of inertia, Vicky reached out for help. The doctors recommended hospice care at home. It was covered by their insurance, and they both felt it was the best way forward. Perhaps a little too soon and too drastic, but there seemed no better solution or help for either of them.

After she settled Carl for the night, she tiptoed out of his room, and before going to bed herself, Vicky thought the day's sudoku would provide some relaxation and tension release. That was the only section of the daily newspaper she bothered with these days. The news was too depressing—she didn't want to add to her angst.

She solved the sudoku quickly, then started on the crossword, until fatigue overcame her. *I'll finish it in the morning,* she promised herself. This was now a regular refrain, "Tomorrow. I'll finish it tomorrow," or, "Tomorrow's another day." There was a time when she derided those who had a *mañana* attitude. Now this had become her *leitmotif.*

Having abandoned the crossword for another day, she finally fell into bed and snuggled there, waiting for Hypnos to come and put her to sleep. She'd learned that exhaustion was an excellent sleeping pill, except on those occasions when tension and fatigue would supercharge her mind and chase sleep away. This particular night, Hypnos won. She needed to rest, to recharge her batteries for the next day.

***

Whatever it is, it can wait till the morning, she told herself as she turned over and tried to get back to sleep. She prayed that Hypnos would return soon. Then she heard it again—and recognized the loud, unmistakable sound of the doorbell with its Big Ben tune. In the stillness of the night, it seemed louder than ever.

In her sleep-befuddled state, she got out of bed and headed for the front door. Then stopped. She quickly turned off the living room light and tiptoed toward the door. The motion light flooded the front porch. Someone or something had triggered it. She slowly lifted the corner of the lace curtain. *Thank goodness I had that metal screen door installed,* she thought.

A man in a short black leather jacket, black jeans, and a large metal cross hanging from his neck stood on the porch. He was waving a cellphone at her and pointing to it as if that was the speakeasy secret code for entry. Not that they had cellphones back in the Roaring Twenties, but this guy seemed to think that his cellphone was his "open sesame" password.

Vicky backed away from the door and waited. Minutes passed, but the man was still there, with the sound of Big Ben reverberating through the house. *Darn doorbell. Why does it have to sound like Big*

Ben? It came with the house and until now she had never thought its sound overwhelming.

Adrenaline coursed through her body. Fight or flight? Her mother-hen protective instinct took over. She couldn't and wouldn't leave her bedridden husband behind. *This idiot, whoever he is, is going to wake up Carl. I don't want him to wake up in the middle of this.*

For once she was thankful Carl was deaf. He called it "hard of hearing," but in reality, he was as deaf as a doorpost. Conversation with him was difficult at the best of times. Even when the tiny aural transistors were in his ears, she had to stand in front of him raising her voice, repeating everything, to which he'd reply, "You don't have to shout, I'm not deaf!" or respond with "What?"

She dialed 911 and asked for the police. She told the dispatcher about the stranger on her front porch. The operator instructed her not to open the door and asked whether the man carried a gun.

"I don't know, and I'm not going anywhere near the front door, because if he is armed he can shoot me through it."

If he's carrying an AR-15, the bullet can pierce the thin metal screen as well as the glass of the inner door. I shan't be able to answer her stupid questions. I'll be a goner.

"Can you describe him? Is he Black, white? How old?" the operator asked.

"From what I could see through the net curtain, he's stocky, with a slight mustache, Hispanic-looking, about 5'8". Maybe in his mid-40s. Please hurry and send the police."

What does she think? That I'm going to ask him to pose so that I can take his picture and then describe him to her? That's all I need just now, she thought. *And if he's armed and I tell her, they'll have to send armed responders and this will take time. I want him gone now.*

She cursed America's love affair with guns. *We went to war in Iraq believing they had weapons of mass destruction, while we allow them in our own homes.* A cocktail of anger, self-doubt, and confusion bubbled inside her.

On top of all the extra work and responsibilities she had to deal with in caring for Carl, she now had to deal with this guy waking her up in the middle of the night. Most probably some drunk or doped-up idiot who had nothing better to do than keep his finger glued to her doorbell. She was both angry and scared.

The operator kept asking her if the stranger had a gun. *She can't be serious. Armed or not I want him gone! How many times is she going to ask me? Am I supposed to ask him? Or tell him: excuse me sir, please keep your finger on my doorbell while I take a closer look to see whether you're armed—the dispatcher needs to know. And by the way, do you hablas español?*

***

Hospice had provided some minimal help in the form of weekly visits from a rotating number of nurses who came and took Carl's vitals. They clucked cheerfully at how well he was being looked after and what a good job she was doing—then left. Vicky was now his sole full-time carer.

As he became weaker and more incapacitated, the hospice assigned Brian to come twice a week and wash him. He was a friendly, no-nonsense person who took his work seriously.

"I love my job," he said. "I like helping people as a hospice aide."

She liked Brian and felt sorry for him because her husband was always difficult and grumpy with him. Most times he'd refuse to be washed and sent Brian away empty-handed. She tried to apologize for him. She did a lot of that lately.

"Oh, don't worry, my dear," Brian said. "I quite understand. They're angry because they can't do what they used to. They feel frustrated and take it out on those around them. You are the punching bag on which he takes out all his anger and frustrations."

"He doesn't realize that if he keeps sending you away, hospice will stop you from coming."

"I know," Brian said. "Patients don't connect the dots because they become the dot—the one and only dot—and can't connect to anything or anyone else."

She looked forward to Brian's visits. His parents had immigrated from the Middle East, but he and his siblings were born in the United States.

"I'm surprised you're not married yourself," she said to him. "People from your parents 'part of the world are keen matchmakers, always on the lookout for a suitable spouse for their kids. How come they haven't found a wife for you?"

"My siblings and I are the first ones to break away from the tradition of arranged marriages," he said. "I'm 32 years old and still live at home. Sad, ain't it? I did have someone in my life for a few years. But it didn't work out. We split up." He sighed. "By the way, I can't come next Wednesday because I have to take a course. We all have to take it."

"What's it about?"

"It's on sexual harassment."

"That's going to be interesting for someone whose job is to bathe and wash people. Let me know how it goes."

***

The unwelcome caller kept pressing the doorbell, as he leaned against the railing. *He's superglued to the spot,* she thought, with fear rising in her heart. He was definitely persistent and determined to gain entry. The house echoed with his ringing. She kept going back to check on her husband, who was still sound asleep, totally unaware of what was going on, as her anxiety gained momentum. Her pacifist tendencies were thrown overboard and, for the first time in her life, she wished she had a gun. *But even if I did, I wouldn't know how to use it,* she thought. She used to joke that she didn't know one end of a gun from the other. "I'd probably end up shooting myself," she told a neighbor who once offered her a gun.

She had good neighbors, but most of them had families and jobs, and at this time of night were sound asleep. When they learned that Carl was ill, they offered to help: "If you ever need anything, call us." But if the guy ringing her doorbell was armed, would they come out and tackle him? Most probably they too would call the police.

The dispatcher told her not to hang up and to stay on the phone until the cops arrived. *Please hurry,* she prayed, while she wondered what she'd do if the stranger managed to break a window and enter her home. How could she defend herself? Kitchen knives? Use the metal meat mallet? What kind of projectile could she throw at him? She didn't even have pepper spray.

Her mind's rotor blades swirled faster and faster, and even her breathing became labored. The operator tried to calm her down by asking questions and keeping her talking—*Where is he now? What's he doing? Don't open any windows or doors*—all prefixed or suffixed with "ma'am," which only added to her fear. Then finally she said: "The police are there now, ma'am. You may hang up."

Big Ben stopped suddenly. Through the window, she saw the stranger go down the steps and walk away. The officers, one male, and one female, stopped him in his tracks. They kept their distance and began to talk with him. She couldn't hear what was being said, but she saw the stranger hand over his phone to the policeman. His female partner stood to one side, hand on her holster. After what seemed like a brief time—perhaps eight to ten minutes—the unwelcome visitor got into his car and drove away. She hadn't noticed his big black SUV, in the dimly lit street, parked behind the bushes in front of her house.

Why did they let him go? She was disappointed that this guy, who had woken her up and brought fear to her heart, was allowed to go free. She'd expected to see him taken away in handcuffs. *That's the least they can do, after what I've gone through.* Vicky was angry as the police walked up her drive. She opened the door.

"Has he gone?"

"Yes, ma'am."

"Do you and your partner need to come in? My husband is bedridden and is fast asleep. What happened? Who's this guy?" She had a hundred questions and couldn't ask them fast enough. The adrenaline was pumping, making it difficult to get her words out.

"No need, ma'am. It was a mistake."

"What do you mean, a mistake? What kind of a mistake? To wake people up at one o'clock in the morning!"

"He was on a nap date."

"A what?"

"A nap date."

"What's that? Some kind of joke?"

"No, ma'am. The joke was on him. He was scammed. He was given this address to meet a woman."

"Is that supposed to make me feel better?"

The officer could see that Vicky was not reassured. She remained agitated and fearful.

"They set up fake accounts and meet people online. They exchange emails and addresses. It's like a chat room. And they decide when and where to meet. He was given this address. I checked it out on his cellphone."

"I'm not that woman. I'm certainly not the kind of person who invites people over for a catnap—or whatever they call it—at this ungodly hour. How many others have been given my address for a nap?"

"I don't know, ma'am."

"And you let him go? You believed his story?"

"Yes, ma'am. It was a genuine mistake."

I wish he wouldn't keep calling me ma'am. Oh dear, he's back.
"Officer, he's come back. He's returning."

Just then a black SUV was seen parking across the street. The officer turned his strong flashlight onto the driver as he was getting out.

"Is your neighbor Black, ma'am?"

"Yes. They are a family from the Congo. They recently rented the house opposite. They're Congolese."

She wondered whether she had to add *from Africa* because he looked clueless. He may have known what a nap date was, but did he know where the Congo was?

"Do you have any family you can call, ma'am?"

"No. We have no family here."

"Any male neighbors or friends who can look out for you?"

"I don't want to wake up my neighbors at this time of night."

"Then I'll go and talk to your neighbor across the street and ask him to look out for you. Goodnight, ma'am," the officer said. "It's all been a misunderstanding."

With that, both officers strode over to talk to the neighbor, who was heading for his front door.

***

Vicky didn't even know the neighbor's name. She felt awkward because the family had moved there recently. She'd gone over with a small cake and found out that they were from Brazzaville and spoke French. And yes, they were Black. She met the mother, grandmother, and their two young children—twins, a boy and a girl. They seemed to be a nice family. The mother explained that the children were learning English. The husband wasn't there when she called. She only saw him fleetingly come and go in his SUV.

She wondered how a Black immigrant man would react when a white policeman flashed a light in his face as he got out of his car. *I don't want him to think that I asked the police to go over and tackle him or bother him. He might think we don't want Blacks in our street. I'll go round with a bigger cake next time.*

How would he feel? She wanted to go out herself and reassure him, even explain, but fear kept her glued to the spot.

Sleep eluded her. She checked all the doors and windows—just in case. Carl was still asleep. She clasped her hands around a cup of hot chocolate and sat in her favorite chair, mulling over the night's events. She castigated herself for being angry with the police officer. He meant well and was trying to help. He even went to talk to her neighbor and ask him to look out for her.

She tried to analyze her feelings. *Was she angry that he took it upon himself to speak to her neighbor, or should she be pleased? I'm all mixed up. This episode has really upset me,* she thought. *I don't seem to be able to think straight.*

For some unexplained reason, her mind went back to a couple of days previously, to Brian's visit, after he returned from his course on sexual harassment.

"How did it go?" she asked him. He described the new norms governing relationships between clients and nurses, patients and doctors, and between any two individuals interacting on a semi-formal or professional basis.

"How many were there?"

"We all had to do it. It was a Zoom course. Just the computer and myself. There are hundreds of us working for this medical group. It was the same for everyone."

"Was it fun?"

Brian rolled his eyes. Then he launched into the new do's and don'ts based on what he called the 'alphabet soup, 'that from now on will, by law, govern most human interactions.

"What alphabet soup?" she asked.

"All that LGBTQIZPR… stuff, whatever they call themselves these days. I can no longer come in and say 'Good morning, Carl 'to your husband."

"Why not?"

"Because that day, he may identify as Carla, or Carrie, or James or…"

"Are you serious?"

"The people who devised this course are, and if I want to keep my license and my job, I have to go along with it."

"Oh dear…"

"And there's another thing. I can't call you or any of my clients 'dear ' because it could be construed as abuse or disrespectful. And I can't refer to Carl as your husband, because you may not be married or spouses. I can't make assumptions. Even if on my instructions docket, you are named as his spouse and carer."

She was speechless. It was crazy, ridiculous, and made no sense to her. It made a difficult job, like his, even more difficult.

"I can't ask you: 'How's he feeling today? 'I have to ask 'How are they feeling today? 'or 'How are we feeling?'"

"You mean use the plural pronoun?"

"Yes. Like there's two of them."

"So I guess you can't coax my husband into the shower because that may be construed as elderly abuse? Or say 'buddy 'to him, because you are not buddies and he may not want to be your buddy?"

"That's right. You're a fast learner."

"Now you're making an assumption, and you're patronizing me by calling me a fast learner." She laughed.

"This craziness is spreading like measles. My sister's a primary school teacher and a six-year-old kept coming to class, one day dressed as a boy—he was a boy originally—and the next day with makeup, painted nails, and wearing a dress."

"Oh wow!"

"The other kids started laughing at him, and his mother complained to the principal."

"What did she expect?"

"Wait for it… the principal then called all the staff to a meeting and told them they should look out and discourage any form of 'bullying' of kids who were trans. The principal said every child 'had the right to experiment with his or her sexuality.'"

"And all this aided and abetted by the mother, who was okay with a six-year-old going through gender dysphoria," Vicky added.

"Yep. My sister said the mom was very pushy, and insisted that her kid had every right to express him/herself. Only, she didn't put it in those terms."

"I'm not surprised teachers, like doctors and nurses, are leaving in droves. They don't want to put up with such nonsense."

"Yes. My sister studied hard and always wanted to be a teacher, but now she's having second thoughts."

***

For some unexplained reason, this conversation with Brian came to mind as Vicky sat drinking hot chocolate at three o'clock in the morning, her hands still shaking, while trying to work out her reaction to the officers 'behavior.

Obviously, the young policeman did not have the same brainwashing as Brian. She remembered that the female officer stood to one side and left all the talking and explanations to her partner. He asked Vicky if she had male relatives she could call. He had even gone over to ask a male neighbor, a stranger to her, to look out for her.

Under the new guidelines, according to Brian, she should have been highly offended that he did that. *How dare he assume she couldn't take care of herself?* He presumed that she was the simple, little woman who needed male protection. *But then, if she could take care of herself and her bedridden husband, why did she call the police? And was the officer wrong in taking that extra step, trying to help?*

By describing the stranger at the door as Hispanic, was she being a racist? Or why did she feel uncomfortable that the policeman shone his flashlight into the face of her Black neighbor? She didn't mind him doing it in the face of her night visitor. Was she catering to her white woman's sensitivity towards Black people—what she called "white man's guilt?" Why did she become angry about the way the police handled the entire incident?

Brian's words came back to haunt her—all this nonsense about political correctness and going overboard not to offend anyone in the alphabet soup created some weird speech and pronoun changes. *Okay,* she thought, *gays, minorities, and women have been marginalized and discriminated against for far too long. Even today there's no pay equity in the U.S. We abolished slavery and yet we still uncover cases of human trafficking and under-waged sweatshops, here and overseas. Now the pendulum's swung too far the other way.*

So... if someone asks me how's your husband, should I now say: "They're OK"? I can imagine the weird looks I'd get. Would that give the impression that I have more than one husband—that I'm a polygamist?

Vicky wasn't sure whether it was the adrenaline or what Brian had said as she began to imagine and weave some ridiculous, even funny conversations. It wasn't only her feelings, but also her mind that was in overdrive. Absurd scenarios came to mind:

"Hi Vicky, how's your son?"

"They're fine, thank you."

"Oh, I didn't know you had more than one. How many do you have?"

"One."

"That's what I thought. How is he?"

"They're fine, thanks."

And all this to avoid the masculine pronoun "he."

Gosh! All this sounds like a fulfillment of George Orwell's prophecy in his book "1984," and we're seeing it in 2023! Doublethink and doublespeak have finally arrived and are being enacted and acted upon. Stop the world, I wanna get off!

The chocolate drink was getting cold, and there were no answers to her questions. *These are imponderables and they'll have to wait. I'll put them on the back burner, or perhaps burn them. All this introspection is keeping me awake. I can't think clearly after what's happened. I'm too tired.*

Tomorrow's another day and I have to take care of Carl. Or will they be Carla?

Christmas With the Penguins

I lost my husband John on Christmas Eve 2023. As the first anniversary of his passing approached, I decided to hit my bucket list. No point sitting at home, feeling miserable. I knew friends would invite me to their homes to celebrate Christmas with them. But at the end of the day, I'd return home—our home—alone. The sadness would envelop me, and so would self-pity and grief.

The most expensive item on my bucket list was a trip to Antarctica. "Why Antarctica?" I was asked. "Because South America and the White Continent are the only places I haven't visited yet," I said. "As long as I have most of my marbles and I'm able to walk and talk, I want to travel and continue to educate myself."

"Bucket List" is a relatively new term that describes hopes and dreams that remain to be fulfilled. This cruise was one of several items on my bucket list. It would start in Argentina and end in Chile with several stops on the way, including Antarctica. Once I told friends where I was headed, I kept getting all kinds of jokes such as: "You've been to both the North Pole and the South Pole—does that make you bi-polar?" Jokes about the Titanic were also included in the jokers 'repertoire. But on the whole, the general reaction was, "Wow, how exciting!" I certainly was excited.

I called my granddaughter Charis in Melbourne, Australia, and asked if she could join me. She was between jobs and jumped at the offer with alacrity. At twenty-six, this was an adventure she could not bypass. She and I would celebrate John's memory aboard the SS Oosterdam in Antarctica, amid ice floes, penguins, and sightings of dolphins, seals, and killer whales.

The cruise company was Holland America. I would fly from San Diego to Buenos Aires and Charis would fly from Melbourne, Australia, to join me there a couple of days before the start of our cruise. I hadn't seen her in fourteen years. When they visited us in the US, she was a pre-teen. Now she was an independent young lady making her way in the world. We were both excited at the prospect of meeting up and making memories together.

We had a last-minute hiccup—more of a panic, actually—as the Holland America representative who got our air tickets booked Charis's ticket to fly from Melbourne, Florida, and not Melbourne, Australia. Big snafu. She knew Charis lived in Oz because I told her so during our numerous conversations. The representative herself had called Charis in Melbourne a couple of times to arrange the flight. At the last minute, she had to cancel Charis's ticket, leaving me to pay at very short notice, during the peak Christmas season. It cost me more than the cruise itself. When I asked the representative why she chose Melbourne, Florida, out of the other four "Melbournes" in the USA, she said, "Because the computer showed that that particular Melbourne was close to Orlando Airport in Florida." I couldn't see what Florida had to do with Australia. She obviously hadn't listened to a word I said to her. And her job was to listen. Her incompetence is beyond words. It caused us much stress and expense.

When traveling, I read reviews and check out the area of hotels where I want to book. Expedia is a great help, and I chose a centrally situated hotel in a safe part of Buenos Aires. Reviews help, and I always make a point of leaving one myself. It was a good choice because many of the tourist sites, monuments, public buildings, and museums were close by.

Seeing Charis again, so grown up and so independent and confident after all these years, was a great pleasure. She was delightful, full of energy and curious about everything. Soon, I realized that I couldn't keep up with her. Her greatest interest was museums and art. She examined each exhibit, read every description on every single floor, and spent hours in one museum before moving on to the next one. In the end, I had to own up and leave her to do her sightseeing while I sat at a local bodega drinking the local vino or coffee, indulging in my hobby—people-watching.

We got on our ship, the *Oosterdam*, on Sunday, December 15th. We stayed docked in Buenos Aires for a couple of days before sailing. Our adventure had begun. I couldn't wait to get to the White Continent—the biggest continent on earth—one and a half times the size of the USA. However, there were many other places to see and explore on the way. We had several stops in other South American countries, as well as the Falkland Islands. All stops offered land excursions with English-speaking guides.

We began our first land excursion in Buenos Aires itself before we set sail. Charis had booked us an eight-hour tour around the Argentinian capital. We had an excellent guide in Valeria who answered all our questions and explained the history of the various sites, monuments, and buildings of interest. Our tour included a visit to the "Recoleta Cemetery," considered to be one of the most famous cemeteries in the world. It contained marble mausoleums in various architectural styles, such as Art Deco and Art Nouveau. It is the final resting place of Eva (Evita) Perón. Valeria explained that the families have to maintain their burial grounds, and if not, the City will raze them to the ground and the next person on the waiting list will grab the spot. There is a waiting list, and apparently, there's also a competition for the best spot! The costs are astronomical.

It's interesting what people will pay for posthumous posterity. This is nothing new. The Pharaohs of Egypt built pyramids, and the Hindus floated their burning dead along the Ganges. Buddhists observed sky burials, where the body is left out for the birds or animals to devour, allowing the soul to depart while embracing the cycle of life. Most of us, the hoi polloi, are happy with a hole in the ground or having our ashes scattered somewhere.

You cannot visit Argentina without hearing mention of the Peróns—Evita and Juan Perón. Just as you cannot escape the mention of their famous beef steaks from cattle grazing on the pampas and tended by the gauchos. They insisted we call them gauchos or rancheros and not cowboys. The word "cowboy" is taboo here. In the UK too, the word has a bad connotation. It refers to someone who is a scammer. Don't ask me why. I have no idea.

Valeria explained that the country is divided over the Peróns 'legacy. Half the country thinks she is a saint, and the other half thinks she supported the autocratic and populist policies of her husband and that they lined their own pockets. There was consensus, however, that Madonna did a good job in portraying Evita in the eponymous movie. According to Valeria, "She did her best." Which I thought was rather condescending.

Our guide had a good sense of humor. Among the many tidbits of information I found interesting was the one about the zoo. As worldwide concern grew about cruelty to animals and the need to protect them in their natural habitats, the Buenos Aires Zoo closed in 2016 and was renamed the Buenos Aires Eco-Park. Most of the animals were moved to nature reserves, but some, those safe to be around humans, were kept on site. The original buildings, enclosures, and cages were converted into bodegas where the denizens sit and sip their wine while the former inmates, now free, roam about staring at the new occupants—a perfect role reversal. It reminded me of the movie *Planet of the Apes*.

I learned Castilian Spanish at school but soon discovered that in South America they speak a different kind of Spanish. It's a sort of dialect with different pronunciations adapted to each country. The hardest for me was Chilean Spanish. They all understood me, but I could not understand them.

The highlight of our eight-hour tour was a meal at a local restaurant that included a tango show. Steak and wine were on the menu. I felt sorry for vegans and vegetarians. I am not a big red meat eater, but the huge steak was tender and delicious. We were told the wine came from local vineyards. The entire restaurant was filled with tourists from our ship.

After the meal, the lights went down and the stage lit up. Three couples posed motionless, poised for the music to begin. Tango music has a strong three-beat sound to it. It has roots in the African candombe, Cuban habanera, as well as waltzes and polkas. It reeks of nostalgia and melancholy felt by those who are far from home. The dance is a statement. A statement of erotica, sexual conflicts, control, and submission. It is quite athletic, and like the flamenco, both dancers hold a strong, aggressive posture and expression—each partner vying for control. Have you ever seen a flamenco dancer smile?

It's interesting what you pick up by way of information while traveling. Mark Twain said, "Travel is fatal to prejudice, bigotry, and narrow-mindedness." In my case, this trip had a steep learning curve. Valeria told us that the tango was birthed in the streets and brothels of Buenos Aires and Montevideo. For a while, it was banned—considered too lewd and crude—until it was exported to Europe. Paris embraced it with great enthusiasm, and it became very popular. After that, Argentina welcomed the tango like her prodigal son and was proud to claim it as her own. If you saw the movie *Scent of a Woman* with Al Pacino, you get the idea.

Argentina was the first country in South America to begin the fight for independence from Spain. The movement gained momentum until each country gained its freedom. However, there are still unresolved border disputes between Argentina and its neighbors—Chile, Peru, Bolivia, Paraguay, and Brazil. When I asked our guide about it, she said, "Sibling rivalry. But when we're attacked from outside, we form a united front." Okay! That's one way of looking at it. I didn't ask her why Chile was on our side during the Falklands War.

Back on the ship that evening, the movie du jour was *Evita*. Unfortunately, I could not see it as it clashed with my line dancing class.

After a couple of days in Buenos Aires, we lifted anchor and sailed east. Our first port of call was Montevideo, the capital of Uruguay. Both Argentina and Uruguay share close economic, political, and cultural ties. The only time they compete aggressively with one another is in sports, especially fútbol.

Charis had booked us a tour around Montevideo, ending at the Museo del Carnaval. Our guide's English was poor, but her enthusiasm was great. Great in telling us that Uruguay was the poor cousin of Argentina and Brazil, where they did everything bigger and better. We noticed dirty creeks and ditches running alongside the main streets. The water was muddy and often filled with debris. I asked our guide, and she said it was part of the Rio de la Plata estuary, which forms the boundary between Argentina and Uruguay. This vast estuary is formed by the confluence of the Uruguay River and the Paraná River at Punta Gorda. *Punta Gorda* means *Fat Point*. The rivers carry a great deal of sediment and alluvial soil from the Andes where they originate.

There is some debate among geographers about whether the estuary should be considered a gulf or a marginal sea. If considered a river, it is the widest in the world, with a maximum width of 140 miles. If you get a trivia question about the widest river in the world, you know the answer now. We saw the muddy freshwater disgorge into the Atlantic until it became engulfed by the ocean's blue seawater. This was even more evident at our next port of call at Punta del Este.

Montevideo stretches along a beautiful sandy beach. We did not see many people crowding the shore or sunbathing. Bondi Beach in Sydney and Rio de Janeiro Beach in Brazil came to mind. Then I remembered that although this was their summer, we were too far south and close to the South Pole for beachwear. There were also hundreds of jellyfish floating close by. That too would be a deterrent. Uruguayans will tell you that the tango was first invented in Montevideo. I just nodded and smiled. I didn't want to start another war between Argentina and their country. Just as I didn't tell our Buenos Aires guide that Argentina won the World Cup in 1986 because Maradona cheated.

Christmas With the Penguins

The main religion of most South American countries is Catholicism. However, there's another religion—fútbol—which is embedded in South American culture and society and is a source of pride and identity. As we drove through the streets of Buenos Aires past the Presidential Palace, Valeria proudly pointed to the balcony where Maradona stood to receive the adulation of thousands after Argentina won the World Cup in 1986. Maradona, Pelé, Messi, and many others belong to the pantheon of fútbol gods. They are role models for young boys—not only in South America but also worldwide. Young lads, while kicking a can down a favela alley, can dream the impossible dream. Some of them succeed. Many fútbol icons come from poor, disadvantaged backgrounds.

Montevideo has many similarities with Buenos Aires—wide tree-lined avenues and houses reflecting their colonial heritage, built in the art deco, neoclassical, and post-modern styles. Our guide said that the local people do not like to live in apartments, but as the city is sprawled along the beach, the only housing is condominiums and apartments selling at exorbitant prices. Montevideo is considered the most expensive city in Latin America. This explains the mass exit of its youth to other countries, despite incentives such as free education starting at primary school and including college. We were told that immigrants from other South American countries, such as Venezuela, help fill the gap.

I was glad that our tour included a visit to their *Mercado del Puerto*. I love visiting local markets, whether indoor or outdoor. It's my way of absorbing the smells and sights of another country. They say you are what you eat, so seeing the type of food people buy to eat gives me some idea of who they are. This market reeked of fish. There was fish and seafood everywhere. I did the tourist bit and took lots of pictures of stalls brimming with sea snails, squid, mollusks, bass, prawns, and crustaceans. Fishing is their primary industry, but there were also other things for sale—fresh fruit, vegetables, bread, and pastries. I limited myself to half a kilo of cherries and some dry papaya. The owner asked me to try them before I bought anything.

Our last stop was at the *Museo del Carnaval*. Carnival is a big deal in Montevideo. It lasts for forty days, from January to mid-March. It's considered to be the longest carnival in the world, and we were about to be given a taste of what it was like. It consists of parades, shows, street dancing to drums, and *murga*, with lots of energetic and noisy fun. *Murga* is a musical style associated with the carnival and it's a uniquely Uruguayan phenomenon. The costumes include exotic feathers and headdresses. They are extravagant and colorful. The dancers move to the rhythm of the drums and invite passersby to join them.

Our show started with three drummers beating on huge drums. The dancers came onstage wearing their bright headdresses and robes. When they finished, they came off the stage and joined the audience. They gave us headdresses and gowns to wear and we followed them, skipping and dancing to the sound of drums around the theater. It was like doing the Hora, but instead of singing *Hava Nagila*, it was more like *Havana*—jump, jump, jump. It was fun, but I found the drumming inside the theater too loud. These people know how to party, but I don't think I can manage forty days of this.

It was time to return home—aka our cabin on board the *Oosterdam*. Over three weeks, Charis and I got used to calling our cabin "home." Holland America calls the cabins staterooms, but we looked upon ours as home, especially after a daylong outing at some port. Once on board, the captain informed us that from now on, we were going to be sailing in the South Atlantic until we reached the Pacific Ocean. Ah, the dreaded Drake Passage. I kept my thoughts to myself as I didn't want to scare Charis, who was already beginning to feel a little seasick. We still had a couple more stops ahead of us before we got to the Falklands—Puerto Punta del Este and Puerto Madryn.

We left Montevideo and headed south to Punta del Este. We arrived there on a beautiful sunny day. Both Charis and I got sunburned as we ambled along the promenade. I was impressed by its wonderful sandy beach and beautiful yachts moored close by. We could not dock up close and personal, as our ship was too big for its harbor. We were ferried there in the ship's tenders. That was another word I learned during this trip—*tender*—not as an adjective but as a noun. A *tender* in boating terms is a smaller boat used to transport people or supplies between a larger vessel and the shore. Some of the smaller ones are also called zodiacs. The *Oosterdam* carried its own tenders. They also doubled as lifeboats. I hoped that would not be necessary, although I did replay scenes of the *Titanic* in my mind.

The promenade had its usual kiosks and ten-by-ten booths filled with local wares to attract tourists. As we poured out of the tenders, they were waiting for us. I admired some of the hand-knitted sweaters made with local wool, probably alpaca and llama. So tempting, but I had to remind myself that living in Southern California, I had no need for them. We walked along the long promenade until my legs told me they were getting tired. I asked Charis to go ahead and explore on her own, knowing she wouldn't be satisfied until the very last tender left for the return trip to our ship.

I mentioned how South America is obsessed with copying and imitating European culture, architecture, and ways of life. Punta del Este is the playground of Latin America's jet set. The city has been variously described as "The Monaco of the South," "The Pearl of the Atlantic," and the "Hamptons of South America." Take your pick. The shore is very scenic and pretty when seen from the sea. The city marks the end of the Rio de la Plata estuary and the beginning of the

Atlantic Ocean. Until now, we'd been sailing in an estuary—a very wide, muddy estuary. From now on, no more muddy creeks. The Atlantic would swallow up the mud and turn it into its beautiful blue-grey, reflecting the color of the sky. The next couple of days we were at sea and were blessed with good weather.

Finally, we arrived at Port Stanley, the capital of the Falklands, on December 22. These islands are an archipelago consisting of two main islands—West Falkland and East Falkland—and 776 smaller islands in the middle of nowhere. They support a population of approximately 3,660 inhabitants who are proud to call themselves British subjects. It is a British Overseas Territory and has a British garrison stationed there. There are many reminders on the island of the 1982 invasion by Argentina and the ensuing war. Argentina lost the war but left behind 20,000 to 30,000 mines. The last of these mines were cleared in 2020, and the islands were officially declared mine-free, thirty-eight years after the conflict. In 2013, a referendum was held and the vast majority of islanders voted to remain a British overseas territory. In case you're wondering—yes, they do drive on the left.

Charis and I boarded a red, double-decker bus for a one-hour tour around the island. The double-decker was obviously imported from the UK. This being such a remote place, I wondered what wasn't imported. The bus driver gave us a running commentary describing the scenery as we drove by. We sat on the upper deck and pointed out to each other the sheep, cows, dry riverbeds, and low shrubs. There are no mountains or forests. Antarctic winds batter the islands, and even the occasional dusting of snow is soon swept away. The land is described by geographers as a desert. It reminded me of the parched, rutted Gobi Desert.

They harvest energy from a few wind turbines and solar panels, generators, and Calor gas. A ship comes every week from Chile (a friendly neighbor who supported them during the war with Argentina) with fresh provisions, fruit, and vegetables.

In the afternoon, we were taken by Len, a fifth-generation Falklander, to the famous rookery. This is located at Bluff Cove Lagoon, where over 1,000 breeding pairs of Gentoo and King penguins lay and hatch their eggs. Penguins mate for life and are excellent parents. The fluffy baby penguins (chicks) stay close to their parents. There was harmonious cohabitation with sheep, cows, flightless Falkland steamer ducks, and geese. We also sighted dolphins and whales in the waters close to the cove.

The rangers told us to keep our distance, but the penguins did not follow that rule. A few came very close to look at these strange two-legged creatures filming them with their cellphones. The wind was quite chilly. We wore our parkas, beanies, and gloves. The penguins huddled together with their chicks resting on their webbed feet or next to them. They made a peculiar noise, like a loud snoring sound. They were adorable. Very cute. I could have stayed there forever, but we had a ship to catch. We appreciated the complimentary cocoa and scones at the Cove's café. Only the Brits know how to make delicious scones. I bought some hand-dyed yarn from local sheep. The islands' income comes from fishing and tourism. Their meat—mostly lamb—fish, and wool are exported to Europe.

The encounter with penguins was the highlight of the trip for me. We still had some way to go, but it was the penguins I wanted to see the most. And I saw them—up close and personal. They came as close as five feet from me. Obviously, they were used to humans and had no fear.

When we returned to our ship, the Captain announced that from now on we were not to consider ourselves tourists, but explorers. I liked the way he phrased it: "As we embark on our journey to the last great wilderness, Antarctica, we're not on an ordinary cruise but on an expedition cruise… It's a rare privilege to witness this frozen world, and together, let's commit to keeping it pristine and unpolluted." The exploration of Antarctica had begun.

We were blessed to have experts on board who gave daily talks and presentations on marine life, topography, climate change, and the type of experiments carried out on our planet's biggest and least known continent. The scientists working there draw from the bravery and experiences of early pioneers such as Scott of the Antarctic, Amundsen, and Shackleton. They hold these heroes as role models for bravery, but also learn from their mistakes. Their findings have far-reaching effects and benefits for mankind—from medicine, botanical science, astrophysics, marine science, and evolution. All the speakers stressed the fact that human carelessness, indifference, and greed have contributed to our climate crisis. They have indisputable data to prove it. Unlike previous cycles of climate change, today's crisis is unprecedented. They point out that Neanderthals did not drive cars, fly planes, decimate forests, or pollute the atmosphere.

In 1959, the Antarctica Treaty was signed in Washington, D.C., by the twelve countries whose scientists worked there. This treaty still holds today for all countries that have stations, explorers, or scientists working on the White Continent. Its purpose is "to demilitarize Antarctica, to establish a continent free of nuclear tests, the disposal of radioactive waste, and to ensure that it is used for peaceful purposes only; to promote international scientific cooperation in Antarctica; to set aside disputes over territorial sovereignty."

Ours is a beautiful planet, and we are its custodians. We have not taken good care of it. If only we could follow the principles set out in the Antarctica Treaty and establish similar treaties among all nations—it would be a more peaceful world.

My Christmas with the penguins was the mental, spiritual, and physical detox I needed. One item on my bucket list has now been checked off, but there are still a few more to go.

Watch this space.

An Epidemic of Loneliness

I heard a moving sermon recently on the subject of loneliness. The preacher talked about how disconnected we've become and how we have a national problem of loneliness. In the last few years, there's been an uptick in articles, movies, talks, and websites dealing with this problem, which is a complex one with many facets and ramifications. It has been analyzed by social scientists, psychologists, historians, and economists.

In 2023, the U.S. Surgeon General, Vivek Murthy, issued a 71-page advisory warning of an American "epidemic of loneliness and isolation." He estimates that social disconnection currently affects more Americans than diabetes or obesity. He said that one in three adults (32%) reported feeling lonely, a significant increase from the previous year. And the data continue to give us increasingly bad news. According to a 2023 Axios/Ipsos survey, 30% of Americans reported feeling frequently lonely. The American Psychological Association (APA) found that approximately 40% of adults feel lonely, with higher percentages among younger adults.

Why this sudden interest in loneliness and its effects on the population? Why not concentrate on some of the many other woes and ills that beset our society? We have wars, hunger, social injustice, racism, poverty—just to name a few. I think it's because loneliness is all-encompassing and pervasive. We are all at the receiving end of at least one of its effects. The government is concerned enough to consider making it a national emergency.

I felt duty-bound to do my own research on the subject. A quick Google search gave me "Googleitis" (my word for information overload). Can I have copyright for that please! Research has shown that loneliness can lead to increased rates of anxiety, depression, and other mental health disorders, as well as early death.

Loneliness is an equal-opportunity player—it affects all genders and all age groups, from baby boomers to Gen Z. The statistics are impressive. A 2022 report by the Cigna Loneliness Index found that 73% of Gen Z (ages 18–24) reported feelings of loneliness, 61% of millennials, and 49% of baby boomers. As for the elderly, it is estimated that 28% of older adults live alone, which also increases the risk of social isolation in this demographic. I think we've had enough statistics to convince us that we have a real problem on our hands.

The sanctification of individualism and self-reliance, the convergence of COVID-19, the technological revolution, cell phones, and remote work are also contributing factors to this epidemic. Add to the mix the political unrest and polarization currently experienced in the U.S., and we have a lethal cocktail that is being constantly shaken and stirred. This is not solely something that's happening in the U.S., but it's a global phenomenon. In Seoul, the South Korean capital, authorities announced that they would spend nearly $327 million over the next five years to "create a city where no one is lonely."

Interesting that they think pouring money into a problem will solve it. We shall have to wait and see.

Pundits have been increasingly concerned with dropping birth rates and increases in elderly populations, both in developed and developing countries. Since the end of World War II, they've been studying and collecting data around this multi-faceted problem.

A healthy civic democracy needs the involvement and participation of its citizens. Becoming involved means you care. Or does it? I remember whenever my mother or any close friend was about to say something negative, they'd say, "Because I care." But caring has become a rare commodity today. What's on the increase is, "Each man for himself." Unfortunately, today we see a great deal of cynicism and mistrust of our governing bodies and institutions, which leads to withdrawal and indifference. There's a prevailing attitude, especially among the young, which says, "It's not my problem. Whatever…" They feel detached and disinterested. Sadly, we have statistics telling us that in 2021 suicide was the third leading cause of death among U.S. high school youth aged 14–18 years. You'd think with all their digital and electronic gadgets they'd have no need to feel life is not worth living.

There are many reasons for these frightening statistics. We can go as far back as the Industrial Revolution when people left their rural lifestyle for city life built around factories. The Technological Revolution was supposed to open the world of knowledge to us via the World Wide Web. Ironically, it has replaced genuine in-person relationships with superficial online interactions. Over-reliance on digital communication creates a false sense of connection while minimizing true intimacy and face-to-face interactions.

We see two people in a restaurant, and they're each engrossed in their cell phones; parents out with their children, and instead of interacting with their kids, they are busy looking at their cellphones. I've also seen youngsters ignoring their companions and playing with their electronics. They do not engage with those around them. Too absorbed in their digital world.

American culture has increasingly emphasized individualism and personal success, sometimes at the expense of community and family ties. This shift may hinder individuals from investing time in nurturing close relationships. We're too busy being busy with busyness.

Screen time increased dramatically during the COVID-19 pandemic. The lockdowns, social distancing, learning, and working from home contributed to this uptick. There are plenty of data proving rising instances of anxiety and depression arising from the pandemic. But even here I see a divide—the kids who were helicoptered around and overprotected, and those who were told to fend for themselves and pull themselves up by their own bootstraps. The latter may not have had boots growing up, but they grew up to be tough. Is that where polarization begins? Does it have socio-economic roots?

Change is constant, so we must also include the changing family dynamics when considering loneliness. This includes divorce rates and delayed family formation (later marriages and fewer children), which contribute to more people living alone and feeling disconnected from traditional family structures. The village is no longer there to help raise the kids. It's the latchkey that lets the kids back into the empty home until mom or dad—or a grandmother—returns from work.

Each era inherits the morals and code of ethics of its predecessors, but it also sculpts its own and often discards those of the past. In my lifetime I've seen the loss of shame. We no longer feel ashamed about things we thought were embarrassing in the past. I remember my mother repeatedly saying: Sit with your knees together. Wear clean underwear in case you have an accident and have to be taken to the hospital. Stand up and give your seat to an old person. Mind your p's and q's. We wear our Sunday best for church. Don't chew gum in public, it's rude.

All these do's and don'ts were there because we worried about how others perceived us. We did not want to create a bad impression. We had a reputation to maintain. We lived among people whom we wanted to think well of us, and vice versa. That was community. We were engaged. Today, the individual reigns. The general attitude is, "I don't care. I don't give a f#%& what they think of me."

Once we disconnect and disengage, the path to loneliness begins. Of course, you can join a group of similar "free" thinkers. But where there are no moral parameters or ethical foundations, the group will disintegrate. This was the experience of the Hippy Movement of the late '60s and '70s. It was an era of free love, free dope, free coupling––a lot of freedom—but it lacked the strong foundations of self-respect, boundaries, and a code of conduct that would keep it together. Utopian ideals and a radical lifestyle were not enough.

In 2000, sociologist Robert D. Putnam published a groundbreaking book titled *Bowling Alone*, based on years of research and data collection. It describes how we've become increasingly disconnected from family, friends, and neighbors, but he also offers suggestions on how we can remedy this. The book resulted in the 2023 movie *Join or Die*, which is on Netflix. It urges us to join in activities and become engaged in our communities, be it churches, political parties, clubs, gyms, or interest groups. Alongside other sensible advice, such as exercise and eating a healthy diet, social interaction is vital for a long, healthy life.

As noted, loneliness is an intergenerational malaise. The younger generations are more willing to talk about their mental health concerns—which was a taboo subject and considered a stigma by older generations. They are still facing a heavy mental health crisis. Again, data speak for themselves—41% of Gen Z and 36% of Millennials said they struggled with their mental health. Both groups have experienced rapid change and have been on the front lines witnessing the epidemic of school shootings, gun violence, assassination of public leaders, 9/11, and Covid. To that, we can also add the current polarization in the U.S. and the wars in Ukraine and the Middle East.

Interestingly, the current emphasis on social integration and respect for hitherto marginalized groups that come under the DEI and LGBTQ umbrellas has created more division and polarization than before. What was intended for good has now been politicized and weaponized. The prevailing "us or them" attitude has increased this polarization. There's no middle ground. This alienates many young people and increases their isolation in today's angry political climate. If grown-ups can't get it together, why should they bother? *Whatever...*

Once upon a time, it was considered bad form to talk about politics, sex, or religion. Nowadays, we talk a great deal about sex and politics, but hardly ever about religion. When I talk about my faith to friends who are not believers, I see that glazed look on their faces as they think: *Whatever. If it makes you happy.* But they do not engage. Is it because they're not interested? Or fearful that they might offend me by having different beliefs or no faith at all? In an increasingly secular world, political correctness can lead to a bland and boring type of discourse. This, too, can lead to isolation and a lack of stimulating interaction. We don't want to offend, so we keep quiet or withdraw from personal or interesting/hot subjects.

An octogenarian friend of mine said, "All my contemporaries have moved away or died. We used to have lively and interesting chats about many subjects. Even heated arguments. In the end, we'd agree to disagree. Now, people are too scared to engage and express themselves. I get text messages from my grands, but nothing of any substance. Just bland chit-chat."

Even though all statistics surrounding the current epidemic of loneliness are pretty depressing, there's good news also. The movie *Join or Die* urges viewers to join clubs, connect with peers, and become involved in their communities, stressing that the health and well-being of the nation depend on it. What's good for the individual, according to Putnam, is good for society as a whole—the common good. Being engaged and involved is good.

Behaviorists maintain that loneliness can be attributed to personalities. Introverts and people suffering from social anxiety, shyness, low self-esteem, sadness, and distrust are more prone to being isolated and disconnected. It becomes a vicious circle. Lonely people have difficulty maintaining meaningful relationships and are less likely to share personal information with their peers. This in turn leads to a lack of intimacy with friends. Some may even be so desperate for friendship that they enter co-dependent and toxic relationships.

Yes, you can be lonely in a relationship where there's no give and take and balanced reciprocity. My friend Lia is one such example. Her husband died recently, and as we were talking, she suddenly said, "You know, I was very lonely in our marriage."

"Really? I always thought you had the perfect marriage. You were always so active," I said.

"That's it! Robert was a homebody. He was happiest doing his projects around the house. He never wanted to go out, or socialize, or have friends visiting. I am a people person, as you know."

"Yes, you were the life and soul of any party we had. We loved having you. And as I recall, Robert was often too busy to join us."

"I kept making excuses for him. In the end, we had parallel lives. He did his thing and I did mine."

This could be true of many marriages today. I think friendships and relationships are like gardens. They need to be planted in good soil, watered, and if need be, gently pruned. But they certainly need care and attention; they cannot be neglected or ignored, or they will wither and die.

Faith is a strong factor in combatting loneliness. When people are part of an organized religion, they generally have a strong social network, which benefits both their physical and mental health. Religion can also be associated with positive emotions, including a sense of optimism and purpose in life, and can provide a healthy coping mechanism for stress.

My churchgoing friend Erica once said to me, "We are blessed to have a strong, caring fellowship and leadership. Whenever there is a need, we try to meet it, whether it's providing meals, spiritual support, financial support, a postcard, a word of encouragement, a telephone call—so that nobody feels left out or isolated."

"Yes, that's good news," I said. "We need more like this, especially in today's climate with all the doom and gloom blasting through the airwaves and social media. We need to have people around us who will share our joys and sorrows."

Pilgrim's Progress by John Bunyan came to mind. The chapter on the "Sea of Despond" left a deep impression on me. The sea was a boggy swamp of deep despair, and the protagonist had to plow through it to reach his destination. Despair often leads to the ideation of suicide. The hopelessness drives people to feel that the only way out is to end their lives.

Humans have an innate desire for connection and fellowship. Christians call their gatherings "fellowship." This is where they chat over a cup of coffee and share what's been happening in their lives. It's a place where they feel accepted without judgment and are comfortable sharing the good and the bad.

Prayer and meditation can help individuals feel connected to God, even in times of loneliness. You don't have to be religious to recite empowering mantras. There is no end of self-help books and advice telling us to love ourselves—to look in the mirror each morning and recite uplifting and self-congratulatory mantras such as: "I'm beautiful," "I'm a wonderful person," "Today is the best day of my life," and many other such uplifting phrases.

These statements are supposed to help us go out and face the world, face our demons, or whatever hinders us from fulfilling our full potential. I've never tried it, so I can't tell if this approach works. Sadly, we have to resort to this—talking to ourselves in the mirror. But these statements would be a lot more powerful and meaningful if they came from our friends and family.

A kind word, a compliment, makes my day.

Grace and forgiveness produce harmony and reduce tensions and stress. Long-held grudges and unforgiveness harm those who hold them. During an interview with Nelson Mandela, the reporter asked him, "Mr. President, when you were released, didn't you want to take revenge on those who had kept you in prison all those years?" His reply was: "I thought about it for a brief moment, but then I realized that if I had, I would still be their prisoner." Indeed, a great man with a great answer. Bearing grudges breeds resentment and makes us bitter. Bitter people are toxic and to be avoided. This, too, leads to isolation.

Building and maintaining friendships is a vital part of combating feelings of disconnection. However, it is also important to be able to disconnect from the noise and many voices around us, which can lead to overload and confusion. Loneliness can drive us to indulge in too much screen time, TV viewing, and online searches—filling the vacuum with a different kind of "noise."

Every time I go out with friends to a restaurant, the noise around me seems to be at deafeningly high decibels. Oftentimes, I can hardly hear the person sitting next to me. Voices seem louder, almost shrill. People talk on their phones in public regardless of those around them, making me an unwilling eavesdropper on their conversations.

As gregarious and outgoing as I am, I also need my space—my time out from all the hustle and bustle. One of my favorite Bible verses is from Psalm 46: "Be still and know that I am God." To me, it means that whatever is happening around us, our ultimate refuge and strength comes from within. If you have faith in yourself or a higher power, you can face whatever life throws at you. No room for suicidal thoughts. Take time out from your busy schedule to meditate, read, think, and relax!

Then go and cook a nice meal for your friends or take some food to someone who is unwell or lives alone. Send someone a card. Write them a nice note. Engage with a neighbor. Go for a walk. Smile at strangers.

Cultivate the Friendship Garden—sow seeds, tend it, and it will yield a great crop.